THE USE OF PSYCHOANALYTIC CONCEPTS IN THERAPY WITH FAMILIES

Other titles in the UKCP Series:

THE USE OF PSYCHOANALYTIC CONCEPTS IN THERAPY WITH FAMILIES

For All Professionals Working with Families

Hilary A. Davies

On behalf of the United Kingdom Council
for Psychotherapy

KARNAC

First published in 2010 by
Karnac Books Ltd
118 Finchley Road, London NW3 5HT

British Library Cataloguing in Publication Data

A C.I.P. for this book is available from the British Library

ISBN-13: 978 1 85575 515 4

Edited, designed and produced by The Studio Publishing Services Ltd,
www.publishingservicesuk.co.uk
e-mail: studio@publishingservicesuk.co.uk

Printed in Great Britain

www.karnacbooks.com

CONTENTS

ACKNOWLEDGEMENTS

Particular thanks to Dr Jeanne Magagna for her significant and exceptional support and wisdom over the last twelve years, and for her invaluable comments on the draft of this book.

Grateful thanks also to former colleagues John Hills, Rosemary Whiffen, and Ann Wynne-Jones for their unique and memorable inspiration.

Ongoing thanks to past and present colleagues in the Department of Child and Adolescent Mental Health at Great Ormond Street Hospital for their daily stimulation, thoughtful creativity, and challenges.

Most sincere gratitude always to all the children and young people and their families with whom it has been my privilege and pleasure to work over the last thirty years: from them I have learned so much.

To
my parents
and my sisters, Gill and Pat,
for being my family

ABOUT THE AUTHOR

Hilary A. Davies was born in West Wales. She has studied at the Universities of Southampton, Kent at Canterbury, and London, Birkbeck College, and also at the Tavistock Clinic and Institute of Family Therapy, London. A qualified family therapist, she is currently working in the Department of Child & Adolescent Mental Health at Great Ormond Street Hospital, London. She lives in north London. *The Use of Psychoanalytic Concepts in Therapy with Families* is her second book; *The 3-Point Therapist* was published by Karnac in 2009.

Introduction

This book aims to be a readable and user-friendly adjunct for therapists working with families who are interested in incorporating into their thinking and practice some ideas from psychoanalytic theory and practice. These ideas are complex, and require as comprehensive an understanding as possible. Clinicians interested in the ideas may also find benefit to their practice from a continuing development of self-knowledge and self-awareness.

It has not sought to enter into theoretical debates about different schools or philosophical positions, for example, on the influence of postmodernism or the technical details of a therapist holding simultaneously both a knowing and a not knowing stance. Some of these discussions have been most interestingly and eloquently written up elsewhere by, among others, Flaskas (1997), Pocock (1995, 1997), and Larner (2000). Nor is the intention to present a book on object relations therapy with families, as this again has been admirably presented by Box, Copley, Magagna, and Moustaki Smilansky (1994), and Scharff and Scharff (1987).

The book also does not set out in any way to compare and contrast traditional systemic family therapy with psychoanalytically informed family therapy, or to present the different schools of family therapy. The presupposition of the book has been that this is a "both–and" model, where the psychoanalytic perspective of internal personal worlds can inform and enhance the understanding of the therapeutic relationship between therapist and family and of family interactions. The terms "therapy/therapist with families" as well as "family therapy/therapist" are frequently used. This is done purposefully both to add variety, and also to avoid any circumscribed and possibly contentious definition of "family therapy" or any assumption that family therapy is somehow different from therapy with families. It is also done in order to include clinicians working with families who are not trained family therapists.

The book does particularly set out to highlight the extraordinary intimacy, intricacy, and intense intra-involvement that is family life. Each child has unique and specific meaning for each parent, and this adds to the rich and complicated mix. The family examples are intended to emphasize this.

Where mechanisms such as projection or projective identification occur in families, there is no belief by the author that such complexities are brought about with malevolent intent by family members. On the contrary, a parent or a child may push out or take on worries or difficult feelings from each other for the purpose of decreasing pain and preserving family life by attempting to maintain a familiar status quo. This they are doing in order to help each other and for the survival of the family as a whole. Although wanting and intending the opposite, parents sometimes unconsciously recreate for their children some of the unresolved horrors of their own past lives, while children are well known for wishing and striving quite consciously to protect and sustain their parents and trying to do everything to keep them together in times of trouble. They may also instinctively wish to keep their parents apart, reserving each for themselves, at times finding themselves in intense rivalry with siblings. Sometimes, they are overwhelmed by this burden and become ill.

For example, parent's best intentions can go awry:

- well-meaning mother helps child over wall into field;
- mother is distressed and anxious as child's ball has blown over wall;
- child is upset and anxious, too, and eager to help mother;

- mother cannot see stinging nettles and Rottweiler on other side;
- child is hurt;
- mother tries to reduce child's pain and repair damage but makes things worse;
- parents take child to professional for treatment.

Therapists always need to keep firmly in mind the best interests of the child. Therapeutic work can be undertaken only in the context of the child's needs and safety being recognized as paramount and where parents are able to meet those needs and ensure safety well enough at all times. The professional's response in the example above would be very different if the parent had helped the child over the wall knowing that there was danger and likely harm on the other side, or if she was being neglectfully unaware.

The essence of therapy with families may be understood as making sense with the family of what has happened. This is not interpreted by the therapist. Rather, the therapist reflects back and comments, through questions and musings, so that the family can create their own interpretations and develop new meanings of use to them. The past, of course, cannot be changed. However, buried feelings and attitudes towards past events can be uncovered and may then be modified and moderated in the interest of present relationships and functioning.

The work is complicated and demanding, and all therapists require a strong supportive colleague group and regular supervision. Psychoanalytic supervision, importantly, considers the experience of the therapist in the therapy as well as focusing on the families themselves, and therapists working with families may gain benefit from this model.

The book does not directly address issues of discrimination or specifically discuss details of race, gender, culture, sexual orientation, class, disability, etc., where prejudice and stereotyping can occur. This would require another book. It is requisite that therapists take fully into account families' and individuals' own descriptions of their particular cultural, political, and social situations during the formation of respectful, helpful, therapeutic relationships. The use of psychoanalytic concepts may need to be modified to embrace varying cultural perspectives on authority and professional relationships.

The family examples in the later chapters have been constructed to illustrate troubled family situations and possible therapeutic responses. No families with whom the author has worked will directly and correctly recognize themselves. The word "parent" has been used as shorthand for "parent or main care-giver" of a child, as it is recognized that some children's primary carer is not a birth parent. The examples are presented deliberately in simplified form, but the difficulties are rarely simple or the treatment quick, as change from within takes time. Sometimes, time frames have been collapsed for the purpose of presentation, and change may appear to have occurred more quickly than it actually would. Hopeful outcomes are generally presented in these examples, though it is recognized that therapy may frequently be lengthy and difficult, with ups and downs along the way, and outcomes are not always clear.

CHAPTER ONE

Psychoanalysis

A brief synthesis of psychoanalytic thinking that spans well over half a century is presented. The main focus on four figures is not intended to minimize the important contributions of others, but does aim to track the progression of psychoanalytic thought from the consulting room of Sigmund Freud out into clinics, hospitals, and community settings from the middle of the twentieth century and on into the twenty-first century.

Sigmund Freud (1856–1939)

The theory and practice of psychoanalysis were first introduced by Sigmund Freud at the end of the nineteenth and the beginning of the twentieth centuries as a method of treating mental illness. He constructed his original theory of psychoanalysis from studying the hidden psychological origins of various somatic symptoms in his patients that were neither explained by physical medicine nor responded to the conventional medical treatments of the time. He developed the practice of psychoanalysis with individual patients, usually adult, and frequently women.

At that time, Freud and his followers were writing for the medical profession and not for therapists. Through his work, he came to understand that beyond a person's observable behaviour, articulated thoughts, and expressed emotions lies something more complex and more profound. He sought to think about and to understand this internal self, and his work took him on from the study of the sick to an understanding of the wider meaning and implications of human behaviour, experience, and relationships. Specifically, he was interested in, and focused his thinking and writings on, that level of a person and personality that was not easily available to scrutiny. Freud called "the unconscious" these layers of a personality structure that exist below what is immediately and consciously experienced by an individual and readily observable by others.

In 1920, Freud presented one of his theories on the nature of the unconscious, that of the repetition compulsion. This theory proposed that, at a very primitive level of functioning, all experience that affects the developing personality tends to be repeated over and over, regardless of pleasure or pain, loss or gain, until there is resolution of the conflict or difficulty. In contemporary work with families, this process might be recognized as a repetition and searching for resolution which may continue over and over and down through several generations (Byng-Hall, 1995). (See Chapter Three, "Influence of early experience in relationships and effect on personality development and later relationships; patterns and myths in families".)

In his patients, Freud observed that buried unwanted memories were often managed in ways that were dysfunctional in adult life, by means of defences: for example, against anxiety (attempts to fend off the memory or unmanageable conflict of feelings) or depression (withdrawal from what is unbearable). In clinical practice, we see children and young people also unconsciously employing dysfunctional mechanisms for coping with unwanted memories, distress, and psychic pain, such as attempting to bury, forget, or deny them. (See Chapter Three, "Defences used to protect the individual against intolerable anxiety or depression, including projection, projective identification, displacement, splitting, identification with the aggressor".) This process can then lead to the symptoms, distress, and ill health that bring children for therapy.

Freud came to believe that unearthing and reflecting on buried memories potentially had a healing effect, and this belief became the focus of psychoanalytic thinking and practice at the time. Freud understood symptoms or dysfunction as developing not only from these defences employed by the immature personality to manage overwhelming anxiety about life events, but also as a failure to resolve early conflicts between different parts of the personality as it developed, with consequent implications for personality development and healthy functioning. In work with families, similarly, we find different family members holding different positions which might equate with different parts of an individual personality: one person being uncontrolled and acting impulsively, with another seeming to be exclusively controlling and repressive. As in therapy with an individual, work with a family moves towards each member managing an integration of the different positions.

Throughout most of his life, Freud's work was directed at seeking to understand and treat what happened in the development of an individual that led to these symptoms causing dysfunction: for example, problems with physical health, emotional or psychological well-being, or within relationships. However, in his later work, he focused more on a theory of "normal" or functional development of the personality through the formation of the "ego" (the mature personality), with the integration of its component parts, the "id" (the uncontrolled and primitive impulses) and the "super-ego" (the controlling and repressive sense of what is good and expected behaviour) (Freud, 1923b).

Some writers have traced one of the earliest recorded practices of family work, maybe surprisingly, to Freud himself. In his work with Little Hans, *Analysis of a Phobia in a Five-Year-Old Boy*, the boy was treated for an apparent phobia of horses. Freud did not work directly with the child, but instead conducted the therapy with the boy through his father as "therapist".

> The case history is not, strictly speaking, derived from my own observation. It is true that I laid down the general lines of the treatment, and that on one single occasion, when I had a conversation with the boy, I took a direct share in it; but the treatment itself was carried out by the child's father ... No one else, in my opinion, could possibly have prevailed on the child to make any such

avowals; the special knowledge by means of which he was able to interpret the remarks made by his five-year-old son was indispensable, and without it the technical difficulties in the way of conducting a psycho-analysis upon so young a child would have been insuperable. [Freud, 1909b, p. 5]

The therapy revealed the source of the child's anxiety as dating to the time of his mother's pregnancy and the birth of his little sister when Hans was three and a half years old. At this time, Hans felt the loss of his mother to the new baby and experienced rivalry for his mother with his father. He felt unmanageable fear and anxiety about the consequences of this competition. Hans's fear was displaced on to the safer object of horses, which could be talked about, whereas rivalry with his father could not be clearly thought about, let alone spoken. He brought to his father descriptions of the feared animals and the circumstances of his fear, which Freud, with the father, understood as Hans's anxiety in his relationships with his parents and about his rivalry with his new baby sister. Through a new understanding, Hans, in time, experienced relief.

In his work with Hans, Freud described his capacity as analyst to allow his own thoughts to follow the patient's associations in order to make sense of the boy's fear. In discussion, Freud writes that the analyst endeavours

... to enable the patient to obtain a conscious grasp of his unconscious wishes. And this we can achieve by working upon the basis of the hints he throws out, and so, with the help of our interpretative technique, presenting the unconscious complex to his consciousness *in our own words*. There will be a certain degree of similarity between that which he hears from us and that which he is looking for, and which, in spite of all resistances, is trying to force its way through to consciousness; and it is this similarity that will enable him to discover the unconscious material. [*ibid.*, pp. 120–121]

Families may also give us hints or insights into unconscious unavailable material through "Freudian slips". These can provide valuable information on the underlying nature of difficulties.

The analytic practice with Little Hans is different from contemporary therapy with families, where therapists work in a room together with family members. However, it is an early example of work with a child being carried out not by an analyst or therapist alone in the treatment room with the child, but by the child's parent at home under the "supervision" of the analyst. It may also be understood as an equivalent to contemporary therapists working in the room with families and utilizing the experience and expertise of parents in order to treat the child.

Through his thinking on what he called the Oedipus complex, Freud presented young children's strong feelings of possessiveness of parents and envy and rivalry with siblings as normal, expectable parts of growing up in a family. As with little Hans, he viewed a sibling relationship as part of the Oedipus complex, where the sibling rivalry is centred around competition for the attention of the parents. The rivalry is not limited to siblings where there is a blood tie, since it exists also in reconstituted families for the same reason of wishing to gain the attention of parents, and may be particularly apparent where one birth parent has been lost. The sibling bond is strong and complicated, and affected by birth order, closeness in age of siblings and gender, differential behaviour of parents towards siblings (actual or perceived), personality traits, and children's life experiences. (See "Family examples", below.) If sibling rivalry becomes extreme, or unacceptably aggressive or distressing, professional help is sometimes sought. (See Chapter Three, "Nature and appearance of unconscious processes, including transference and countertransference, the Oedipal stage, and free association"— "Oedipal stage".)

Most often, Freud's way of working with his patients was directly through the relationship developed intensely over time in the therapy room. Within the therapeutic relationship, the patient's uninhibited expression of thoughts (through free associations and recounting dreams) was available to the analyst's understanding (interpretation). The technique of interpretation as a therapeutic tool was one of Freud's earliest contributions. (See Chapter Three, "Importance of interpretation and containment".)

Importantly, also, patients developed a dependence on the analyst that allowed the analyst to understand aspects of the patients' relationships with their parents or primary care-givers in infancy from the nature of the patients' relationships to the analyst in therapy (transference). The analyst's own personal response to this transferred material (countertransference) was also included in the interpretations back to the patient. This way of working, through the therapeutic relationship with patients' unconscious material and past experience as manifest in present relationships and current defences, is a distinguishing feature of psychoanalysis and psychoanalytic psychotherapy. (See Chapter Three, "Nature and appearance of unconscious processes, including transference and countertransference, the Oedipal stage, and free association".)

Freud's work was influential in moving professional thinking from a focus on symptoms to an emphasis on the central importance of primary family relationships and, in analysis, on the relationship between analyst and patient. He worked with his adult patients through their formative relationships being "transferred" on to the relationship between analyst and patient in the consulting room. Now, therapists with families are working in the therapy room directly with young people and their families and their current relationships, which include also internalized models from past relationships.

Melanie Klein (1882–1960)

Following Sigmund Freud, Melanie Klein began her work in 1919 and developed further Freud's ideas on the workings of the inner world. She was particularly interested in the idea of innate aggression, developing this from Freud's theory of the death instinct (Freud, 1920g). Alongside this, she presented her idea of the centrality of love as a basis of life. She came to focus on the conflict between love and the more destructive feelings of hate, guilt, and aggression, and saw the resolution of this conflict as crucial in the development of the functioning personality (Klein, 1937). In Freudian terms, Klein thus considered the childhood struggle between the superego (what the child believed he or she should do or feel) and the id (the child's natural desires or impulses), with attendant anxiety in the formation of the functioning ego (the integrated personality). The analysis or therapy worked to provide the safe therapeutic space and relationship that offered sufficient containment and understanding for the conflict of feelings to be recognized and thought about, and for defences to be no longer required.

Melanie Klein applied Freud's theory of psychoanalysis to the practice of child analysis. She recognized the role of play in the analysis of children, where play in a child may be thought of as the communication equivalent of free association in an adult. She also saw play in itself as being therapeutic for a child, who could play out over and over again current inner unconscious conflict until some relief was experienced. For example, loving mummy and daddy, but feeling murderous hatred when they are together and the child is excluded. Though the play itself was felt to be therapeutic, the analyst might also offer interpretation or understanding of the unconscious feelings, fears, conflicts, and defences expressed in play by the child. In this way, the child experienced that overwhelming anxiety or conflict could become both bearable and available to being thought about and understood, with the aim of providing relief. Similarly, in family meetings, with the contribution of the therapists' understanding and containment of feelings, the families' facilitated conversations can in themselves be therapeutic. (See Chapter Three, "Importance of interpretation and containment".)

In her development of play technique with children, one of Klein's basic beliefs was that all play has symbolic significance. She realized the importance both of having a clinical space separate from the child's own home for the conducting of the analysis, and of each child having his or her own individual box of toys which was used only for the treatment with that particular child and which was left closed in the therapy room after each session, ready for the next. In this way, the child experienced security and containment of conflicts and anxieties with the therapist and within the therapeutic setting.

Klein contributed ideas on "splitting", which many therapists with families will recognize. For example, a father may be marginalized and reported as being "useless" and "never there", with mother taking all responsibility, or the child who is the identified patient may be described as "the whole problem", with other children in the family being presented as having no difficulties at all.

Splitting is recognized as a part of usual development. Infants hold on to and benefit from the "good" experiences (those that feel positive and manageable) and initially project the difficult or "bad" experiences into parents for them to process and manage for them.

A young infant will enjoy and grow from the pleasure and comfort of the mother's presence. However, initially, the infant will experience unmanageable rage and distress at the mother's absence. At first when this occurs, the infant needs to split off the scary angry feelings into another person who provides containment through comfort, holding, and reassurance, and who bears and processes the feelings so that they are not overwhelming. For example, the infant screams in panic when mother is not there, mother arrives and holds, talks to, and reassures the infant, the infant quiets. Without the presence of the containing other person, the infant is likely to become swamped as the panic takes over. In time, from a repeated experience of the "bad" projected feelings being held and made bearable, the infant is able to internalize the good holding experience and manage the difficult feelings him- or herself.

Therapy with families where splits are presented would work both towards recognizing and acknowledging the function and dysfunction of the splits and towards integration of the "good" and the "bad": for example, bringing together and recognizing both the positive contributions and difficulties of mother and father, and of all the children in a family. This can be achieved within a family structure where all family members can, for example, express their aggression and more "negative" feelings, such as rivalry and envy, as well as the "good" and acceptable ones. (See Chapter Three, "Defences used to protect the individual against intolerable anxiety or depression, including projection, projective identification, displacement, splitting, identification with the aggressor"—"Splitting".)

Anna Freud (1895–1982)

At about the same time as Melanie Klein, Freud's daughter, Anna Freud, began her work in developing the ideas of her father for the analysis of children. In 1927, she published her first writing "Introduction to the technique of child analysis". She paid tribute to her father as the source of her own ideas and work, and acknowledged that they felt they were the first to understand human behaviour and its difficulties as originating not in overt factors, but from the pressure of instinctual forces coming from the unconscious mind.

Just before the outbreak of the Second World War, the Freud family fled from Austria and settled in London in 1938. Sigmund Freud died soon after the war began. Following her father's death, Anna Freud continued to explore in her work the effects of the war on children who had lost a parent through death or separation, such as evacuation away from home. In London, she founded the Hampstead War Nurseries, which provided care for children of single parents. The children were encouraged to develop attachments through continuity in their substitute care, and by parents visiting as often as possible. With Dorothy Burlingham, Anna Freud published her studies of these children during wartime: *Infants without Families* (1944) and *Young Children in War-Time* (1942). Before her move to London, in a nursery set up for the poor of Vienna in 1937, Anna Freud, together with her colleague Dorothy Burlingham, had begun observations of infant behaviour. Following the move to the UK, Anna Freud continued this work, first at the Hampstead War Nurseries and then at Bulldogs Bank, a home for orphans. She believed that, as much as possible, the parents should be involved with their children, and her observations included interactions of children with their parents.

Anna Freud wrote of children whom she observed also in daily situations and ordinary life environments, such as mother and toddler groups, nursery schools, and baby clinics. For her book *Normality and Pathology in Childhood* (1965), she drew both on her experiences in clinical practice at the Hampstead Clinic (founded in 1952) and on observations of children and babies in community settings, developing an understanding of their play. She noted the repetitious use by children of defences whose function and origin needed to be understood. (See Chapter Three, "Defences used to protect the individual against intolerable anxiety or depression, including projection, projective identification, displacement, splitting, identification with the aggressor.") She observed and emphasized unproblematic development also in order to understand developmental difficulties. These observations became studies on child development and then the basis for Anna Freud's teaching and training courses, which later developed into the child psychotherapy training at the Hampstead Clinic (now the Anna Freud Centre).

In addition to her important development of observation of infants and children with each other and also in their family interactions, throughout her life and work Anna Freud aimed to find useful applications of psychoanalytic ideas and theory in daily life and ordinary family settings outside clinical consulting rooms. She contributed this thinking also to the areas of the criminal, family and child care law, children's rights, and education.

Donald Winnicott (1896–1971)

Following on this work of Anna Freud, a significant contribution by Donald Winnicott throughout his career and in his writing during the 1950s and 1960s until his death was also to bring the ideas and practice of the psychoanalytic treatment room further into "the outside world". He trained and practised as a paediatrician, followed by qualification in the 1930s, first as an adult analyst, and then as a child analyst.

Donald Winnicott belonged in what became known as the object relations school, which emerged out of the ideas of Melanie Klein and her "paranoid–schizoid" and "depressive" positions. Object relations theory developed the idea that a child moves on from an early stage of total subjectivity, where everything outside the self exists only to meet the needs of the self, importantly including the child's primary parent. At that early stage of development, the young infant has no awareness of those outside having any exis-tence other than to meet his or her needs.

Winnicott and those in the object relations school of thinking were particularly interested in the stage of development when a young child becomes aware of the other-ness, or separateness, of the world around him or her and of the people in that world. Dependent upon a "good-enough", "facilitating environment", the child moves on to develop a growing capacity to relate to others in the outside world, in order not only to have his or her needs met, but also to find an acceptable social place in the world among other people.

So, the child moves from an exclusively "subjective" experience, where everything outside exists only to serve his or her needs, to a growing awareness of others, objects outside the self, having an independent existence and validity. This awareness is followed by the child developing ways of positioning him- or herself in relation to the outside "objects" and forming reciprocal relationships with them. In this way, a sense of self in relation to others is developed.

In considering and working with the young and growing child's capacity and ability to develop relationships, Winnicott thought both about what is helpful to the child in this and also what is essential. Through this thinking, he developed some of the ideas and concepts for which he is best known.

Donald Winnicott's "holding environment" is the child's context of a supportive primary relationship. For example, this relationship between child and mother allows the child safely to move from total dependence and immersion in the mother through stages of increasing autonomy and independence.

The "good-enough mother" is one who is able to provide the thinking presence and containing relationship for the child that is sufficient for this task.

A "transitional object" is an object that is imbued for the child, when away from the presence of the mother, with the essence of feelings of safety and security with the mother in the past. It serves the important function of holding the child through these times. Transitional objects may be rags, blankets, or soft toys, which, importantly for the child, are often not washed, presumably with smells and tattiness contributing to the general sense of history and well-being derived from these objects.

> It is not the object, of course, that is transitional. The object repre-
> sents the infant's transition from a state of being merged with the
> mother to a state of being in relation to the mother as something
> outside and separate. [Winnicott, 1974, p. 17]

In his work as a paediatrician, Winnicott was interested in the interplay between psychological and physical ill health and was concerned about the psychological effects on children of hospital admissions. With his wife Clare, a social worker, he worked from 1941 during the war with evacuated and troubled children in Oxfordshire. In hospitals and evacuee hostels, working with social work and community colleagues caring directly for the children, Donald Winnicott developed his thinking and work with children and young people in community settings, using ideas from his psychoanalytic trainings.

Summary

The teachings, theories, and work of Sigmund Freud, Melanie Klein, and Anna Freud, and maybe Donald Winnicott also, may, in many ways, seem remote and removed from the experiences and difficulties of children and families in an inner city, multi-cultural, contemporary, twenty-first century world.

However, the work of these early forerunners has been built on and developed by succeeding and contemporary psychoanalysts whose thoughts now about clinical stance in relation to their patients is not so far removed from modern family therapy thinking of working alongside, and in collaboration with, families. In therapeutic work with families, similar difficulty as for individuals can often be identified as occurring at times of expected major transitions in a family's life, or in response to particular trauma or loss. This can be understood in families as emanating from family members' varying responses to the requirement for change or adjustment. It can also be recognized as originating from unresolved or unacknowledged disagreement between family members about change or no change, or about the nature of change. Difficulties in families around transition points may also be organized by unmanageable anxiety experienced by the family as a whole about unknown and unwanted consequences of any change and the inevitable losses. This can result in impossible attempts by the family, or else by individual members, to preserve the status quo, sometimes leading to family distress or conflict, or to ill health.

As each child moves through developmental stages which present issues that can become crises if not sufficiently understood and supported, so transitions occur for families as a natural developmental process. For example, a major task in the first year of life is the development by a child of trust in others. The task requires the responsiveness of a parent to the needs and distress of the child. When the appropriate response is evoked repeatedly, the child experiences relief, learns that his or her needs will be met, and the child can move on. If the child experiences a lack of response to needs and distress, the child continues to seek the required response and remains held in this stage of development (Fahlberg, 1994). A continuing lack of trust by the child can lead to crises, for example, at the time of starting nursery or school, or later in a child's life behaviour may become increasingly challenging as the young person continues the search for a reassuring response. (See, for example, Chapter Seven.)

By examination of some psychoanalytic theory and concepts, and by relating these ideas and insights to the difficulties of families who present with mental health problems in children and young people today, the following chapters will aim to demonstrate and illustrate the potentially productive common ground.

CHAPTER TWO

Therapy with families and family therapy

The East London Child Guidance Clinic was founded in London in 1927 by the Jewish Health Organisation. It was the first child guidance clinic in the UK and, reportedly, also in Europe. It was set up to meet the needs of the immigrant population who had settled in that part of London since the beginning of the century and whose children were perceived to have emotional, psychological, behavioural, and educational difficulties requiring this kind of service.

In 1929, the London Child Guidance Clinic was opened in Islington, North London. The Foreword to an early report of this clinic is quoted as saying that "in its efforts to adjust the groping child mind to life, to make useful citizens of difficult and abnormal boys and girls, [it] is doing the work of civilisation" (www.starcourse.org/emd/posthuma.htm). The Clinic was able to offer a service to almost 1900 children and families from all over the UK in its first 4½ years of existence. The Clinic later moved and became the Tavistock.

In the early years of child guidance clinics, social work was a key clinical intervention, with the involvement of the children's families being regarded as most important. The founding honorary director of the East London Child Guidance Clinic was Emanuel Miller, who is quoted as writing in one of the Clinic's early reports,

> Experience has stressed the importance of understanding the role the family, the grandparents, and uncles and aunts play in the problems of the child. The grandmother is, for example, often found to be a potent force, perhaps a hidden one in the family affairs, and until her attitude to them is disclosed it may be found impossible to make headway in the elucidation and removal of the child's difficulties. [Renton, 1978, p. 311]

This thinking may indeed have heralded the beginnings of more formal family therapy, which was to develop and make its mark during the latter decades of the twentieth century. However, it also highlights a significant subsequent change in therapy practice. In some cultures it has more recently become concentrated primarily on the nuclear family and, due to economic, political, and sociological influences on family life, rarely on an extended family, which has become more geographically dispersed across wide distances.

So, in the 1950s in the UK and outside the clinical analytic setting, psychoanalytically orientated individual casework began to be developed and more widely practised in the community and also within the burgeoning provision of child guidance clinics. Contributions from psychoanalytic thinking that were increasingly recognized and employed included: early family experiences as they affect present functioning; unconscious motivation; possible coherent meanings of apparently irrational thoughts and behaviour; defence mechanisms; and inner conflict and ambivalence. These all served to illuminate the casework task. "A prime tool in subsequent treatment was a 'corrective' emotional experience through the relationship with the caseworker" (Younghusband, 1981, p. 29).

After the traumas and upheavals of the Second World War, and as individuals looked for greater security and comfort, increasingly the nuclear family became the cornerstone of a new-found social stability in the following decades. In the UK, the work of John Bowlby on the importance of infant attachment to the mother was widely influential at this time when women were being encouraged back into a central role in the home and out of the factories and

workplaces to make way for the returning men. Bowlby emphasized specifically both the importance for each child of having a
primary carer/attachment figure and also the enduring influence of
early experience.

With this developing central role of the family in social life there
appears to have arrived also an increased expectation of harmony
within the nuclear family. Individuals began to look at their
emotional lives and relationship satisfaction in a new and more
demanding way. Expectations had changed from a mere wish for
survival to a hope of comfort, well-being, and also of happiness. For
the first time, problems or unhappiness experienced by children
were looked at differently, now within their family contexts, and
parents were sometimes called to account for their children's difficulties.

In this new era, it was no longer considered that children in
distress could be taken from their social contexts, away from their
families, to be treated and cured alone by a therapist or analyst in
a distant clinic room. The effects of separation on children were
becoming more widely recognized through the war-time work of
Anna Freud and Donald and Clare Winnicott, the ground-breaking
films of John and Mary Robertson in the 1950s (Robertson, 1952),
as well as from John Bowlby's understanding of children's attachments. For many, the real effects of separation through bereavement
or evacuation during the war had been felt at first hand. Increasingly, parents and families were to become included in professional work with children experiencing emotional, behavioural, or
mental health difficulties.

While keeping some connections with family-based social casework, and at the same time moving towards a family-orientated
approach to individual difficulties, family therapy began in the
USA in the 1950s and developed during the 1960s and 1970s on
both sides of the Atlantic. It was interesting that the early family
therapy forerunners and pioneers developed a theory evolving not
so much from its psychological precursor, psychoanalysis, but
instead turned for their theoretical base to sciences, such as mathe-
matics, cybernetics, and biological, behavioural, and communication sciences (Bateson, 1972; Watzlawick, Bavelas, & Jackson, 1967).
However, many of the early family therapy practitioners were
psychoanalytically trained.

Following Laing's idea of the illness-inducing power of families or parents, such as the schizophrenogenic mother (Laing, 1971; Laing & Esterson, 1964), some early family therapy writing looked for the origin and maintenance of a child's illness within family relationships (Palazolli, Boscolo, Cecchin, & Prata, 1978). At times, causes for difficulties were identified within family patterns where relationships were found to be "dysfunctional", mothers "enmeshed" and fathers "disengaged" (Minuchin, 1974). So, family therapy was initially generally developed according to a medical model of therapists gaining information and observing families, diagnosing, and prescribing. The families were mainly recipients of this process. Minuchin later changed his position significantly "the more expert I become, the more I can experience being wrong. I am an expert in uncertainty" (Clark, 2004, p. 43).

In 1979, Walrond-Skinner acknowledged that: "Laing and his associates have been extraordinarily influential in developing an intellectual climate conducive to viewing psychological disorders from within a framework of dysfunctional interpersonal relationships" (p. 4). This influence did work to promote systemic thinking in relation to individuals' difficulties. However, it also suggested that ill health developed in the context of family relationships that were not working and needed to be fixed, rather than that these relationships might be functioning well but had been subject to unusual circumstances or overload that required professional help and that the relationships were central to the solution.

In the UK in the 1970s and 1980s, multi-disciplinary child mental health teams came together to think about children and young people within their family context. These professional teams kept the family and its dynamics as their focus, with the purpose of treating the problems of individuals by working with the family as a whole. A number of clinicians from the Tavistock Clinic, Great Ormond Street Hospital, and the Institute of Family Therapy in London recorded the development of their thinking and practice (Bentovim, Gorell-Barnes, & Cooklin, 1987). Their initiatives included setting up a self-training programme that went on to offer formal family therapy training from the 1980s.

As this formal training developed in the UK in the 1980s and 1990s, family therapy, along with other disciplines, was becoming influenced by postmodern ideas. The effect of this influence was a movement away from professional expertise and certainty, diagnosis, and prescriptiveness towards the development of shared partnerships between therapist and families with a growing emphasis on families' own expertise in their search for solutions. An important influence in this movement was probably the creation of the multi-disciplinary teams which brought together thinking from a number of different professions. Also, there was, by this time, an increasing number of family therapists who either were or were becoming dually qualified both as family therapists and as psychoanalysts or psychotherapists. This increase in psychoanalytic thinking among family therapists brought differences to the practice of family therapy including: increased openness and acknowledgment of uncertainty; greater emphasis on the importance of relationship between therapist and family; and the development of a co-constructionist model with the possibility of creating a shared view and understanding with the family.

In 1997, the *Journal of Family Therapy* devoted an entire edition (volume 19) to "Psychoanalysis and systemic approaches". Some contributors to that edition were either qualified or becoming qualified in both family therapy and psychoanalysis. Some had already written on the inclusion of psychoanalytic ideas in therapy with families and the importance of the therapeutic relationship between therapist and family (Flaskas, 1997; Pocock, 1995, 1997).

Now, in the new millennium, though perhaps for different reasons, psychoanalytic thinking and individual psychoanalytic psychotherapy with children and young people may be viewed still with reserve and caution within some multi-disciplinary child and adolescent mental health services. This form of treatment is time- and therapist-intense, as individual psychoanalytic psychotherapy requires regular appointments at least weekly and may continue over a significant period of time. This form of therapy may appear less amenable to rigorous scrutiny by some of the more conventional methods of research. It might, thus, be concluded that it is particularly complicated and challenging to promote and develop individual psychoanalytic psychotherapy as an evidence-based treatment. Importantly, its use of the therapeutic relationship and the experience and feelings of the therapist in the transference and countertransference may be unfamiliar to the more numerous therapists trained in behavioural, cognitive, or systemic forms of therapy and their research methods. Similarly, therapy with families that incorporates ideas and concepts from psychoanalysis may also be considered difficult to research. This could be different if methods were developed to incorporate more practice-based research and practice-based evidence.

A different approach to audit and research will be needed if the effectiveness of psychoanalytically-based therapies can be assessed equally and take their place in listed evidence-based practice. Qualitative and narrative methods of research will need to be used increasingly and developed creatively.

The following chapter will focus on specific aspects of psychoanalytic thinking and practice, encompassing ideas and techniques first presented and developed in Vienna in the early 1900s, with a view to identifying their applicability and relevance to current thinking and practice in therapy with families within contemporary diversified cultures and societies.

CHAPTER THREE

Psychoanalytic theory, concepts, and practice with families

Introduction

I t may still be curious that psychoanalysis is referenced very little in some of the seminal family therapy literature recommended when formal family therapy training was first set up in the UK in the 1980s and 1990s.

Prior to this, as noted above, and when family therapy thinking was beginning in the mid-1950s and the theory, teaching, and practice were initially developed during the 1960s and 1970s, there may have lingered some residual uneasiness about psychoanalytic theory and practice and its digging into the murky underlayer of the human psyche, beyond observable human behaviour and interactions. They may still have been thought to belong mainly in the analysts' consulting rooms for use with individual adults and increasingly with individual children also, and to be less applicable to work and therapy with families.

Some early family therapists, such as John Byng-Hall and Carl Whitaker, did incorporate psychoanalytic thinking into therapy with families. However, many initially moved away from these concepts based on working with internal personality structures and relationships between therapists and families towards therapy focused more on observable interpersonal relationships, behaviour, and interactions as they were experienced or described in the therapy room.

From a psychoanalytic perspective, clinical treatment is a joint task carried out in the dynamic relationship formed and developed between client and analyst. Within this relationship, analysts use transference and countertransference, and an understanding and interpretation of free association or undirected play to seek to illuminate the client's situation and distress. Analysts work with their patients on conflicts between love and hate and other destructive feelings, and on incapacity to bear and contain psychic pain (Bion, 1962, 1967) as the major obstacles to psychological growth and functional development. They work towards an ability to regulate emotional responses (Schore, 1994), to mentalize (Fonagy, 2004), and to create a coherent account of emotional experience as being necessary for psychological health. (See "Affect regulation, emotional communication, and 'mentalization'", below.) By bringing the difficulties to conscious awareness, they become available to shared reflection in the process of working towards relief and recovery.

A basic belief of psychoanalytic thinking and practice is the universality of strong innate feelings, such as love, hate, envy, etc., leading to dilemmas and conflicts within individuals and in relationships, whose resolution is fundamental to healthy development.

Family therapists have relied little on their transference and countertransference experience in the room. Nor have therapists with families generally focused on seeking to understand the unconscious processes of individual family members or of the family as a whole. These concepts form the cornerstone of psychoanalytic practice and may be helpfully applied to work with families also. Therapists with families do work with the therapeutic relationship and the therapy space as containers for the families' conflict of feelings, in a way similar to that of psychoanalytically trained colleagues with individual patients.

Psychoanalytic theory may also inform thinking on therapy with families in order to increase the possibility of understanding, and thus working with, the individual experiences and processes that lie behind what is observable and more immediately available. Some clearer insight into the particular conflicts, defences, personality structure, and relationship styles of individual family members might lead towards greater clarity on the relationships observable in the room and on reported difficulties. This may lead to greater understanding of the contribution by individuals, past and present, to collective experiences and beliefs that have led to the formation of particular family thinking and interactions which may have become stuck in unhelpful or problematic ways.

As graphically expressed by Michael Nichols,

> If people were billiard balls, their interactions could be understood solely on the basis of systemic forces. The difference is that human beings interact on the basis of conscious and unconscious expectations of each other. However impossible it may be to understand people without considering their relationships, it is equally impossible to understand those relationships if we think only of external behaviour without considering internal realities. [Nichols, 1987, p. x]

So, therapists working with families may benefit from an increased awareness not only of what is said or demonstrated by families, but also of unexpressed meanings, feelings, and anxieties. This could be supported by knowledge of ways of communicating thoughts and feelings that are not explicitly and overtly presented: for example, via the transference and countertransference, and different defences. (See Section "Content", below.) Psychoanalytic theory can help therapists to recognize underlying defences that give meaning to what might otherwise appear to be insignificant and unimportant material. It can also support therapists in understanding and respecting the strength and purpose of both individual and family defences and resistance as a part of, and not in contradiction to, the therapeutic process. These serve a protective purpose until anxieties can be sufficiently contained.

In work with families there exist the family equivalents of the individual analytic relationship. Family therapists develop a complexity of relationships and several combinations of therapeutic connections: (1) to the family as a whole, (2) to relationships within the family, and (3) to each individual family member.

The therapist's tasks include helping and enabling the family to develop together the capacity to think and to communicate about difficult emotions so that they can work towards safely giving up defences against unmanageable pain that have stood in the way of development and progress. In this way, families are supported in adapting and managing life's transitions and challenges without the family or any of its members becoming psychiatrically, psychologically, emotionally, or psychosomatically unwell.

Within the therapeutic relationship, the therapist and family together aim to achieve this by working towards the verbal expression of difficult feelings and aspects of relationships, the effective negotiation of ever-changing relationships as children develop and grow up and families move through life stages, and the naming of the un-nameable in the easiest possible way, with the aim of managing the most available and least painful changes that will make sufficient difference to the functioning and well-being of the family as a whole and of each family member. The therapist will benefit from a knowledge and understanding of individual processes, pain, fear, anxiety, ambivalence, conflict, the complex nature of defences, and the positive effect of containment in order to do this.

From psychoanalytic theory, we understand the importance of the integration of the different parts of the personality in the development of the mature functioning person. Similarly, in families, individual family members may hold different characteristics for the family: for example, father is the strict and rational one, mum is soft and emotional, big brother is challenging, and little sister is perfectly behaved. This blend may work until a life transition or family crisis occurs. Then, as in the well-integrated, functioning individual personality, the family members will need to manage the different assigned characteristics flexibly in order to adapt to the new challenge.

For example:

- dad loses his job and needs to work away from home for a while;
- big brother's challenging behaviour will become out of control if mum cannot take on a bit of "strict" in dad's absence;
- little sister is distressed at dad's absence but cannot show it because she is the perfectly behaved one, and she may become physically unwell.

Or, if mother is less emotionally available for a while because of bereavement, the children might struggle with their upset and worry about this if dad were unable to help by taking on a bit of "emotional" during this time.

A number of questions arises.

1. How are therapists working with families, differently from individual therapists, able to achieve the balance in intervention between the needs of the individual family members and of the family as a whole?
2. How do family therapists, who are not required to have any of their own individual analysis or therapy as part of training, gain sufficient self-knowledge and insight to manage safely a complexity of relationships, so that they are able to see and meet the needs of families distorted as little as possible by their own personal experiences, and sometimes by an apparent need for authority and expertise? And how can they be guided by what the families bring ahead of their own experience of relationships and family life?
3. What is the family therapist's role in working with unconscious processes?
4. In what way and to what extent can knowledge of the transference and countertransference be present and helpful in family therapy? If so, how can it be used by family therapists who have not, of necessity, experienced their own therapy?

Process

The process is what happens in the therapy room in the relationship between therapist and family together. In therapy with families, as in psychoanalysis with individuals, emphasis is placed on the safety and predictability of the therapeutic setting. The reliability of both therapist and setting allows the patient to develop trust in the therapist and in the therapeutic process. This experience of security with a reliable therapist allows the exploration of emerging feelings together. So, the aim is to provide this safe, containing, holding space within which the troubles and conflicts of the family can be explored. This may take some time.

Time and place

The importance of the absolute regularity, consistency, and reliability of time and setting in psychoanalytic practice is generally recognized as being equally central in therapy with families. Therapists may be guided by some important psychoanalytic principles in setting up and conducting meetings with families.

In individual psychoanalytic practice with both adults and children, the principle is well established of using the same room for each session and of meeting on the same day(s) and at the same time on each day consistently every week. The purpose of this in analytic practice is to allow the development of the transference relationship between analyst and client so that the transference and countertransference material can be used and interpreted in the analysis.

Therapy with families is different, as these therapists are not necessarily trained to develop, understand, and interpret the transference and countertransference. However, therapists with families may helpfully use the psychoanalytic principle of a safe, reliable, prepared and predictable time and place within which a relationship can be developed between therapist(s) and family which is central to the process of working towards the recovery of the referred child.

In family therapy, that would mean that for each meeting each week, where possible but not inevitably, the same room should be used. In busy, overcrowded clinics and hospitals, this may not always be possible. Unlike individual psychoanalytic psychotherapy, for family therapy meetings it is acceptable if necessary to change rooms, provided that a "room within a room" is created and prepared in advance. This "room within a room" comprises a set of chairs placed in a circle of, preferably, the same size for each meeting, forming a contained and predictable space within which the dynamic relationship between family and therapist(s) can occur and develop. (See Chapter Five, "Clara".)

The therapist(s) may choose to discuss and decide with families whether or not it is important regularly, or on certain occasions, to place chairs in the circle for absent family members also, or for those (for example, siblings) who attend the meetings but do not attend every session.

Equally, as family therapy meetings are usually deliberately more spaced out in time than individual psychoanalytic psycho-therapy meetings (that is, family meetings usually occur at weekly or fortnightly intervals), a variation in the time and even the day of meeting is not necessarily disruptive in the same way that it might be in individual psychotherapy. In therapy with families, the thera-pist needs to take account of the demands on the time not only of him- or herself, but also of a number of family members with work, school, family, social, and other commitments. A rule that the meet-ings need to be at exactly the same hour on the same day each time might thus work against the engagement between therapist(s) and a number of family members in a productive therapeutic relation-ship. Some flexibility, therefore, may be helpful within the reason-able expectation that family meetings happen unfailingly and predictably, barring unforeseen or unavoidable events, at agreed intervals: for example, each week or fortnight.

A sole therapist would be fully trained to conduct therapy with families and would take the lead if working with a co-therapist who was not fully trained. The co-therapist could be a junior colleague or trainee gaining clinical experience within this safe setting. The co-therapist would learn within the therapy room from the trained therapy practitioner and could also explore and develop their own style and confidence in this protected setting.

Formation of relationships between therapist and family

In this model of therapy with families, informed by psychoanalysis, of central importance is the development in the room of the dynamic relationships of therapist with the family as a whole, and also with individual family members, which begins from the very first meeting. These relationships are formed by the therapist connecting with the family as a unit, with particular family rela-tionships, and also with each family member, with recognition of individual experience and feelings. The relationships continue to adapt and evolve over time and provide the safe therapeutic context within which change can occur.

As a reliable room or setting provides an important contained and predictable physical space, so an open, accepting, non-judge-mental, and assumption-free therapeutic stance by the therapist in relation to the family can provide a creative and productive psychic space. The therapist's stance may actually be more important in the therapy than any specific family therapy school.

Such a therapeutic relationship, formed using principles from psychoanalytic theory, would require the therapist to be comfortable and skilled in an open and enquiring approach, in each session being receptive to the family's agenda and worries, and to the family's own report of successes and difficulties. The therapist would need explicitly and genuinely to have processed for him- or herself and eschewed any preconceived ideas about family life or causes of difficulties. He or she would need truly to approach the family and each therapy meeting with an open mind, free of any templates or formats for the process of therapy with the family, or of any ideas about how families should be. Included in the therapist's role and task with families is an active avoidance of any increase of the family's feelings of blame, hopelessness, and despair, while at the same time seeking to decrease these unhelpful feelings. The therapist aims to promote and enhance the parents' sense of effectiveness as parents in helping their child to get well. This may be an equivalent of the work to strengthen healthy ego functioning in psychoanalytic practice.

For example: parents of Mary, twelve, who has an eating disorder, report that they have been unsuccessful in their attempts to feed her over the past week; they feel useless as parents and responsible for her low weight.

Therapist: "You are doing extremely well in helping your daughter cope with her worries about eating sufficiently to maintain her weight at present, [indicating two healthy younger siblings] you are clearly such successful, competent parents, and Mary's current illness does not change that. We can think a little more together about how Mary would like you to support her over the next week." (*Helpful facilitating response.*)

Therapist: "We are worried about Mary's lack of weight increase and wonder what you [addressed to parents] need to do differently. We noticed that she was able to eat her snack here with us today, but you cannot get her to do this at home. Perhaps we need to think more about your own difficulties [addressed to parents] which may be affecting your ability to support your daughter." (*Implied blaming comment.*)

At the same time, the therapist facilitates a developing family conversation in which the referred child is supported in finding a voice. In this style of therapy, the therapist has no preconceived or privileged knowledge or information on what is optimum functioning for any individual family. However, he or she, first and foremost, is skilled and experienced in facilitating, processing, and developing to best advantage what each different family brings, and in supporting families' strengths in moving to their own individual solutions.

This relationship between therapist and family can then provide a place where the unsaid and previously unsayable can be aired and where risks can be taken. The therapist offers safety, containment, and a new and hopeful understanding of what has formerly been unbearable to speak and to share. The therapist aims to offer informed processing and a shared different meaning to the developing conversation. This resembles, though is also different from, Melanie Klein's idea of the mother as reliable and predictable container and digester of the infant's confused and unmanageable feelings, which are then restored to the infant in safe, processed, and manageable form. (See Chapter Four.)

This stance by the therapist exemplifies a basic tenet of family therapy practice, the "neutrality" of the therapist, described in 1980 by Palazzoli, Boscolo, Cecchin, and Prata. This could equally be a description of the clinical stance of the psychoanalyst or psychoanalytic psychotherapist. The final sentence of a brief quote on "neutrality" may also have been written by a psychoanalytic clinician of their own open-minded, non-partisan stance: "In fact, it is our belief that the therapist can be effective only to the extent that he is able to obtain and maintain a different level (*metalevel*) from that of the family" (p. 11). Regardless of debates about neutrality, both in therapy with individuals and with families, what is of importance to the patients is the reflective presence of the therapist who maintains a meta-position from which he or she is able to convey that the feelings of the patient are experienced and can be thought about. The meta-position does not inhibit connection with the patients' emotional experience, but, importantly, does protect the therapist from being overwhelmed and enables him or her to maintain a thoughtful responsiveness. The meta-position or meta-level is at one remove from the discussion and can be described as one from which the therapist comments on, rather than participates in, conversation. For example, the therapist does not take part in an unproductive discussion about a family holiday, but observes to the family that they are having difficulty making a decision and wonders about that.

Content

Potential contributions by psychoanalytic theory, concepts, and practice to the thinking and practice of therapy with families include the following.

1. Influence of early experience in relationships and effect on personality development and later relationships; patterns and myths in families.
2. Ambivalence and conflict.
3. Defences used to protect the individual against intolerable anxiety or depression, including projection, projective identification, displacement, splitting, identification with the aggressor.
4. Nature and appearance of unconscious processes, including transference and countertransference, the Oedipal stage, and free association.
5. Importance of interpretation and containment.
6. Affect regulation, emotional communication, and "mentalization".

While therapy with families may be considered and practised within a psychoanalytic framework and using psychoanalytic ideas, such psychoanalytic techniques as interpretation and transference and countertransference are inevitably considerably modified for use in therapy with families (Lanyado & Edwards, 1997).

Influence of early experience in relationships and effect on personality development and later relationships; patterns and myths in families

In every nursery there are ghosts. They are the visitors from the unremembered past of the parents, the uninvited guests at the

christening. . . . Even among families where the love bonds are
stable and strong, the intruders from the parental past may break
through the magic circle in an unguarded moment, and a parent
and his child may find themselves re-enacting a moment or a scene
from another time with another set of characters. [Fraiberg,
Adelson, & Shapiro, 1975, p. 387]

Psychoanalytic thinking and literature pay specific and helpful
attention to the special importance of childhood experience in
personality formation and to the significance of the past in deter-
mining subsequent behaviour.

While the nature/nurture debate will continue, environment in
a child's early history is accepted as being an important factor
contributing to the development of the child's ego strength, that is,
to the integrated, functioning personality that will develop ways of
managing life's transitions, losses, and inevitable challenges and
stresses. For healthy and age-appropriate growth and development,
a child has certain specific needs, such as reliability and consistency
from the primary parent who makes a central and essential contribution to a young infant's nurturing environment.

When a child's early care and environment are secure and satis-
factory, an individually developed pattern for managing impulses
and for dealing with frustration and difficult feelings is built up
over time and integrated into the child's growing personality
(Winnicott, 1970).

This positive early experience makes possible what Melanie
Klein called good "internal objects" (Klein, 1975). This refers to the
internalization of a positive nurturing experience which enables the
developing child to trust and believe in him- or herself and also in
other people, and so to develop strategies for dealing with difficulties. Signs of ego strength, or a healthy functioning personality
structure, include an ability to manage, for example, anxiety, guilt,
loss, envy, change, and sadness. Its lack is indicated by an absence
of these coping abilities and a tendency to be overwhelmed by
anxieties when faced with even ordinary day-to-day demands,
uncertainties, and pressures.

Sigmund Freud emphasized that the roots of emotional life and
development lie in our experiences in infancy and early childhood.
He also explored systematically the connection between events and

possible emotional traumas of these early years and the structure and functioning of the later personality.

In "On the psychical mechanism of hysterical phenomena: preliminary communication" (1893) Breuer and Freud wrote of the potential long-term effect of earlier "psychical trauma" which is not effectively processed:

> We must presume rather that the psychical trauma—or more precisely the memory of the trauma—acts like a foreign body which long after its entry must continue to be regarded as an agent that is still at work. [Freud & Breuer, 1895d, p. 6]

In contemporary child and family mental health interventions, it has come to be recognized and accepted that the separation of a young infant from the primary parent after an emotional relationship and attachment have been formed is likely to be damaging to the child's emotional and personality development. This is understood in the resultant arousal of distress, confusion, and, sometimes, even apparent hatred in a young child when the parent is felt to have withdrawn and be no longer available. The child experiences this as abandonment and the neglect of his or her emotional requirements and need for love. In reality, this situation may have been caused by an actual physical separation for different reasons, such as a parent leaving the family home either briefly or else permanently. Alternatively, the separation may be the perception and experience of the child that he or she has been rejected, abandoned, and/or superseded (for example, by the birth of a sibling). Such trauma may continue its effect in adult life and into parenthood, if unrecognized and unresolved through the creation of an account of the emotional experience and the development of a psychic structure that can recognize, feel, and think about it.

Professionals in child and family mental health services or in social services departments are regularly faced with emotional and psychological difficulties, not only in the children who are referred but also in parents. The unresolved difficulties of the parents, often traceable back to their own early years, may have exacerbated or contributed to maintaining those of their children. This happens frequently, and often as much work needs to be devoted to supporting the parents in addressing their own emotional issues, emanating from past childhood experience, as in helping the children directly. This process is different from situations where there are child protection concerns possibly requiring investigation, because of persistent, recognized, and avoidable harm caused to a child by a parent. (See Chapters Six and Seven.)

> But where commonsense action by the parents to deal with a problem in their child's development seems to be impossible, one almost always finds some unbearable event in the family. Discovering and understanding all this strengthens parents' ability to change things in the present. [Daws, 1995, p. 65]

Professional intervention may be indicated for some families in order to interrupt a pattern of one generation following another into neglect or emotional or psychological difficulties, with apparent inevitability. Britton (1978), among others, has written of an intergenerational "cycle of deprivation", where intervention at a critical point seems essential in order to break the cycle and prevent the problems of the past being passed on to the present and future generations (p. 374). In the containment of meetings with the therapist, families can find a safe thinking space in which to develop the psychological structure and strength to begin to reflect on their emotional experience and difficulties and to construct a coherent account.

> Freud has postulated the process of *working through* as an essential part of psychoanalytic procedure. To put it in a nutshell, this means enabling the patient to experience his emotions, anxieties and past situations over and over again both in relation to the analyst and to different people and situations in the patient's present and past life. [Klein, 1959, p. 297]

The italics are original, though the phrases "working through" and "talking through" are now a standard part of therapeutic language. In clinical therapy, the "working through" with families of past difficulties as they continue in the present can protect a child from carrying issues for the family at the expense of his or her own healthy functioning. (See Chapter Eight.) The "working through" refers to the family's developed inner capacity to think about issues by looking at the past in the context of present unconscious patterns of relating.

Patterns in family relationships

Therapists work with unconscious internal family relationships as they interact with external family dynamics. This means, for example, working in the room with a couple where each has internalized a model of the father as assertive and the mother as passive and ineffectual; the couple relates to each other in the present according to this model, and so re-create the relationship that each has internalized from the past. This has led to problems for their son, who sees his mother as ineffectual while she sees him as aggressive and a problem.

People may choose partners in line with family scripts of what is expected, both consciously and unconsciously. The pattern of family relationships can be orchestrated by what partners carry and manage for each other in the splitting which occurs in the couple. For example, father owns the aggression and mother denies her own aggression, which she projects into him rather than challenging and getting into conflict with him. Family structures may lack a place in which the aggression in all family members can be acknowledged. So, some children may then be viewed as perfect and no problem, and others as aggressive and the "bad", troublesome ones. Therapy will work towards all family members being able to own their aggression and more negative feelings and to express these in some way, so that more troubling hostile feelings can be parcelled out and the family work out conflicts between them rather than locating the "badness" and "problem" in one member. In this way, disagreements and conflicts are acknowledged and discussed and mother and father can be supported in feeling closer as a couple after being able to express some of their mutual aggression.

Myths in families

In clinical practice, the therapist and family together work to connect with and think about the family's past and present family myths, beliefs, and intergenerational scripts and customs which are stored in current unconscious family dynamics. These are considered as they interact with real present situations. Sometimes, a family tree is drawn together in the room.

Family myths have been thought about as the equivalent in families of defences in the individual (Byng-Hall, 1981; Ferreira, 1963). Referring to Ferreira, Byng-Hall writes of family myth, "He defined it as the pattern of mutually agreed, but distorted, roles which family members adopt as a defensive posture and which are not challenged from within the family" (Byng-Hall, 1981, p. 105). These roles may also "reduce the family's flexibility and capacity to respond to new and unrehearsed situations" (*ibid.*). Indeed, all families probably have myths, which are firmly held beliefs about themselves derived from current unconscious thinking about the family. However, the function of the myth is to preserve the roles assigned to members and to protect the status quo. If circumstances require a different response, inflexible roles determined by the family myth may prevent a necessary developmental course of action. This shared defence is constructed in family systems to sustain the familiar and defend against new challenges that are frightening and, the family fears, might lead to some unknown disastrous consequence.

For example, a family fears that, if a parent who is believed to be vulnerable is challenged in any way, he or she will become depressed. The myth is that challenging certain people leads to depression. This may have been true of family members in the past; it may or may not still be true in the present, but it is believed to be so. The myth is helpful in terms of protecting the parent and avoiding disaster. However, it leads to all other members being silent for fear of upsetting the vulnerable parent, and contentious issues do not get discussed or sorted out. Also, if circumstances change, for example, if the coping parent is suddenly unavailable, unless the other parent is able to bear the challenge and be uncharacteristically coping and supportive of the children, the family may move into a crisis. Inflexible myths and roles can be an impediment to healthy functioning and development.

Ambivalence and conflict

Psychoanalytic theory offers an understanding of aspects of human behaviour as resulting from conflict between interacting or opposing impulses—the familiar experience of being "in two minds" about something. Perhaps these are what Sigmund Freud called the "id" (what I want to do or feel like doing) and the "superego" (what I think I should do, or what I think is the right thing to do, or what I think someone else, probably a parent, wants me to do). In children and adolescents, as well as in adults, the inability satisfactorily to cope with and resolve such conflicts may lead to emotional or psychological distress or illness.

A psychoanalytic perspective may enhance an understanding of the role and contribution of ambivalence in parenting difficulties.

> . . . unfortunately, coupled with these delicious and loving feelings there comes all too often . . . an admixture of resentment and even of hatred. The intrusion of hostility into a mother's, or a father's, feelings for the baby seems so strange and often so horrifying that some of you may find it difficult to believe. Yet it is a reality and sometimes a grim reality, both for the parent and for the child. [Bowlby, 1989, p. 17]

A parent may experience great relief if the therapist expresses understanding and acceptance of conflicting feelings, and explains that contrary emotions of love and hate can exist side by side without the presence of one negating the other. The feelings, acknowledged by parent and therapist, can then be examined and worked with. (See Chapters Four, Six, and Seven.)

It may emerge through the therapy that the ambivalent feelings of the parent have their origin in the parent's own childhood. An experience of deprivation in childhood may lead to interrupted emotional development and to a difficulty as a parent in expressing love and affection, or, alternatively, to an overwhelming urge totally to possess a child's love. Also, for a parent, a childhood experience of jealousy on the birth of a sibling may lead to resentment of a new baby in adult life. A parent whose love for his or her own mother was, for example, characterized through childhood by attempts at resistance to her controlling ways, may find these feelings resurfacing as resentment and even hostility to the perceived or actual demands of their own newborn child. (See Chapter Six).

The difficulty lies not so much in the existence or recurrence of the old ambivalent conflicting feelings, but more in the parent's lack of understanding or ability to manage them. Parents can become confused, distressed, and frustrated at not being able to be the unfailingly loving and devoted parent that they would wish to be and believe that they should be. This may bring back memories of their own experience of inadequate parenting, as they struggle to parent their child in the way that they recall their own parents struggling and failing in their childhood. More important is whether or not they have developed the inner psychic capacity to manage and think about feelings in relation to these internalized relationships from past experience.

For example, a father who received physical punishment as a child resolved not to be violent with his own children. However, his internal model of a violent father and terrified child remains with him unresolved: he identifies still with the child and avoids any form of authority that is like his father's. He walks away from his young sons when they are challenging, rather than risk becoming his brutal father. The children's mother colludes with this approach, because she is aware of his temper. The boys are left with no limits to behaviour and at risk.

More than anything, parents do not want to fail as their own parents did. The therapist with the family recognizes and acknowledges the nature of these confused feelings and supports the parents to develop the capacity for thinking about how their experience in the past is present in their parenting of their own children now. The therapist provides the secure safe place within which this difficult and painful conversation may be possible.

Bowlby writes,

> ... the mother who is constantly apprehensive that her baby may die is unaware of the impulse in herself to kill it and, adopting the same solution she adopted in childhood perhaps in regard to her death-wishes against her own mother, struggles endlessly and fruitlessly to stave off dangers from elsewhere—accidents, illnesses, the carelessness of neighbours. The father who resents the baby's monopoly of his wife and insists that her attentions are bad for it is unaware that he is motivated by the same kind of jealousy as he experienced in childhood when a younger sibling was born. [Bowlby, 1989, p. 18]

Sometimes, a parent, and also professionals, may be extremely concerned by the strength of the ambivalent feelings towards a child, so that the parent may need a separation for a while, and this may happen. If the child is cared for elsewhere, the parent's sense of inadequacy and guilt may increase, as may the levels of hostility between parent and child. Informed and insightful assessment and therapy with the family requires an understanding and acknowledgement of the parent's conflicting feelings, including both hopelessness and rejection, and also a strong wish to be a good, loving parent. If, through professional anxiety or lack of understanding, only the former were recognized, the latter could be lost, leading to potentially disastrous consequences for the child. (See Chapter Seven.)

Difficulties for a child, who has struggled with a conflict of feelings in coming to terms with abandonment by a parent through parents' separation or divorce, are not always clearly recognized and acknowledged. These may sometimes be expressed indirectly: for example, through physical, psychosomatic, or psychiatric illness. (See Chapters Eight and Nine.)

Defences used to protect the individual against intolerable anxiety or depression, including projection, projective identification, displacement, splitting, identification with the aggressor

Therapy or analysis, compared, for example, to counselling or psycho-education, includes work with the patient's or family's defences. Defences serve different purposes. They can serve a positive, functional purpose, and can also stand in the way of necessary, desired change. They protect against change, because the familiar, though unpleasant or dysfunctional, is experienced as preferable to a step into the unknown, even when the family are saying strongly that they want and need something to be different. Or defences guard against the feelings of hurt and loss involved in change, which can be difficult and painful, again when the familiar is left behind. An everyday example is some people's resistance to wearing new clothes, even when they know that the old clothes are no longer functional and the new ones look much better. The familiar can often have an attraction and give a sense of security and an illusion of well-being, sometimes in subtle and unrecognized ways.

Defences against unbearable and unresolved conflicting feelings may stand in the way of change that seems very difficult and overwhelming when feelings of anxiety and fear have not been sufficiently contained. ("Will someone laugh at me with my new clothes?" "Will someone feel envious and steal my new cap?") The degree of difficulty in moving on can be significantly compounded by defences that are built up over time to protect the individual or family against what is too painful or difficult to face, or perhaps just frighteningly unfamiliar. (For example, denial: "I didn't really want a new cap, the old tatty one is fine", or ". . . the old one was useless anyway.") If "friend/partner" is substituted for "cap", the intensity of anxiety can be appreciated.

Resistance may also result from a strong superego (controlling sense of good behaviour), which creates too much guilt for other behaviours and feelings to be thought about. For example: a child has envious feelings towards a newborn sibling but feels such guilt that only good and loving feelings are expressed.

People employ defensive strategies to protect themselves against anxiety caused by changes or challenges in external reality and by inner stresses or pressures from internal conflict. Sigmund Freud, Klein, and Anna Freud all contributed to an understanding of the use of defences against conflict and anxiety.

At times of particular anxiety and unmanageable conflict of feelings, a child may use "regression" to an earlier time when life was more manageable and the world seemed safer, more protected, and less demanding. At the birth of a sibling, small children may manage their confusion of emotions of hate and envy, as well as love, by taking themselves back to a time when life was more manageable and reverting to earlier behaviours, such as soiling or tantrums. A five-year-old may become again more clingy to mother when faced with the anxieties of beginning school. In context, these behaviours can be understood, but, if they persist, they may become problematic.

Overwhelming impulses, distress, or fears can also be dealt with by means of "rationalization"—finding a justification for the forbidden instinctive behaviour or reaction to a perceived outside threat. The perceived "threat" may simply be the possibility, or indeed immediate offer, of something different, such as a new job or relationship, or a move of home.

Melanie Klein wrote of the important defences used by infants and young children, including "splitting", "projective identification", and "introjection". Defences may also include "denial" and "repression", used in order to believe that difficult and painful problems do not exist, or "contempt" to minimize the importance of something that cannot be faced. It is the absence of secure containment, which allows the development of an effective inner psychic structure, that necessitates the use of defences.

For example:

- the frightened boy becomes a bully as he is unable to manage his anxious feelings of vulnerability if he does not first become the aggressor. (See Chapter Seven: "Billy".)
- a mother projects into her child aggressive feelings which she has not recognized or found a way to express as her own. (See Chapter Seven: "Greg".)

Family myths may serve the same purpose for families as defences do for individuals (Ferreira, 1963). These may be directly implicated in resistance to change at important transition points in the family life cycle. They may also be involved in the family's conscious or unconscious avoidance of any change of view of life events or of individual family members, past or present. (See "Influence of early experience in relationships and effect on personality development and later relationships; patterns and myths in families", above). An entrenched family myth may enable a family to continue to "split" the good and the bad. In this way, they may perceive an ousted family member as a scapegoat who carries all the causes of difficulties in the family, so that present family members can be freed of any part in family problems. This may lead to difficulties for the family in recognizing, managing, and resolving problems as they occur and in safely negotiating the challenges of developmental life stages.

Importantly, the different defences do not operate in isolation from each other, but may overlap and interact to a significant extent. Also important is an understanding that these defences are perceived by the individual or family as being life-supporting or life-enhancing, and are felt to be crucial and fundamental to the person's, or family's, survival and well-being. The therapist respects defences, since a direct challenge is likely to be met with resistance, counter-attack, or flight. Defences can be recognized, respected, and acknowledged as having a real purpose, and together therapist and family can look at safe and agreed ways of moving on.

Of particular importance to the family therapist is not so much a detailed knowledge of the various possible defence mechanisms, but, rather, an awareness of these processes used regularly by individuals and families to protect against, for example, anxiety and conflict which may be involved in the process of change. An understanding of the kinds and sources of anxiety against which individuals or families may react and defend is a central area of knowledge for children's and families' mental health professionals (Timms, 1964). Within the emotionally secure experience of the therapy, family members can be supported in the room to observe and think about their beliefs, interactions, and ways of dealing with conflicting feelings, so that defences may be safely relinquished.

Projection

Projection describes a process where difficult feelings or parts of the personality belonging to one individual are pushed out, or projected, on to another person or other people in the individual's external world. These projected parts are then seen as belonging to someone else and their source is not acknowledged.

For example, a father may come home from work in a bad mood because of something that happened at the office that day. He is feeling cross and upset but is finding this difficult to express openly, or even to acknowledge to himself. Normally, he is a coping, cheerful person, who is seen by his family and by himself as big and strong and dealing with everything. On arrival home, he rushes in and falls over the dog, who is lying sleeping in the hallway. Father shouts crossly at the dog, who then wakes up and barks loudly. The father shouts at the dog, who barks more loudly. The youngest child of the family gets cross and upset because the dog is distressed, grumbles at father, who then shouts at the child for being cross and upset. Father shouts to mother to sort out the child, who seems to be "in a bad mood, all cross and upset for some reason". The "cross and upset" is thus moved along or "projected" from the father into the small child, via the sleeping dog. Even if the young child had not displayed "cross and upset", the father would have identified the feelings in the child and not in himself. Father then sits down quietly with a drink and a newspaper while mother sorts out the "cross and upset" child.

It is not difficult to see that if this scenario is played out a number of times, the young child might easily come to be seen as a cross and upset child. The child may then become a problem or target area for the family's difficult emotions and a repository for the unrecognized and unmanaged feelings of others. (See also "Projective identification", below.)

In therapeutic family work, the source of the "cross and upset" (father) would need to be traced and recognized and the feelings owned and expressed appropriately, for this tangle of passed-on emotion to be unravelled. Further work might then be done on family stereotyping (for example, father as the "coping, cheerful . . . big and strong and dealing with everything" one), and on family styles and methods of emotional communication. Work would also be done with the family on allowing and supporting family members in owning their own feelings, particularly when being cross and upset seems unmanageable.

Another example is a mother who reports her child as distressed whenever the health visitor visits. The mother might be projecting and seeing in the child her own feelings of distress and anxiety. She finds this way of avoiding experiencing and acknowledging her own difficult feelings, but her child's behaviour is then identified as troublesome. It is important that professionals recognize that the mother's description of the child's feelings may sometimes, in fact, be a way of communicating her own.

Some of the most problematic parent–child relationships, which lead to serious difficulties for the child, may originate in the parents projecting on to the child a difficulty that they are not able to recognize and manage in themselves. It is important for professionals and therapists to be aware of this possibility when they see children with difficulties, reported or observed, which seem to be stereotyped, fixed, or irrationally intolerable to the parent.

The therapist can focus on the parent's internalization of early experience that has been re-triggered in the current parent–child relationship. The parent is supported to consider his or her own experience in the areas that are currently problematic between parent and child. In this way, the parent can be helped to convert projection into greater understanding.

For example, a professional can acknowledge to the young mother, above, her understandable anxiety about visits by the health visitor, because of feeling under scrutiny and fearing that she may be found wanting. This may allow the mother to acknowledge her worry, which then may be reduced.

From the perspective of a young child, unwanted or unmanageable feelings may be projected on to someone in the outside world to whom will then be attributed all sources of frustration and distress.

For example, when roused to fury, a child may put all his loving and caring feelings into his mother so that he can give himself over totally to the experience of anger and rage. Or else the child may project all his angry feelings into the outside world in order only to experience the more manageable and less scary feelings of being good and loving; if this continues, the child might then become anxious and frightened about this hostile and scary outside world, with consequences for his place in it. Adolescents may be holding and expressing the unarticulated protest of their parents as well as for themselves, while the parents hold and express the more reasonable and thinking parts; the oppositional and more amenable parts need to be held within each family member, rather than one holding the aggression and others the reason and maturity.

Britton gives an example of the use of psychoanalytic understanding with deprived children:

> Analytic work with such children has shown how hardness, apparent indifference and apathy are the means of avoiding the terrors of vulnerability and dependence, and how cruelty and ruthlessness are used to rid the self of mental pain by inflicting it on others. The awakening of the belief in genuinely good relationships dependent on someone else's quality is felt to be a threat to a whole personality structure or system of pseudo-independence or hardness . . . To come closer to such children, therefore, is to evoke powerful and disturbing emotions and to raise hostility. This leads to many breakdowns in well-intentioned efforts by foster parents. [Britton, 1978, p. 376]

This gives a different meaning to the behaviour of violent and anti-social adolescents. Young people who have had unreliable carers will feel danger at the possibility of dependence and vulnerability within a caring relationship for fear that they will again be let down. Their hardness and apathy protect them from this possibility.

Children's play may contain both projection and much indirect communication of the child's inner feelings or experience. These uncomfortable feelings may be attributed to imaginary people, dolls, or objects: it is then these objects who are upset, worried, or naughty and may do or think wicked things. This projected play, if understood and contained, can be therapeutic for the child, who can in this way act out safely some overwhelming inner feelings. At the same time, this can give the therapist a clearer view of the nature of the child's true feelings. This can form an important part of therapy meetings with families where young children may play or draw while the adults talk, and the child's play information can be incorporated into the therapy. (See Chapter Seven, "Billy".)

Family members who are unable to bear emotional pain and self-examination may manage these feelings or situations by arousing them in others: for example, in their children, also in therapists, and sometimes in the different agencies involved.

Projective identification

As with "projection", projective identification can be understood as either a defence mechanism or a means of communication, or both. It is an unconscious process where feelings that are felt to be unmanageable are disowned by arousing those feelings in another person ("projection") and where the other takes on the projection by identifying with it. The projector can then identify and respond to the feelings in the other person ("projective identification").

Melanie Klein explained the emphasis of projective identification as being on the acquisition of some characteristics of the "external object" (or other person) and on taking them into oneself sufficiently to be influenced by them (Klein, 1959). She maintained that both projection and introjection are features of the early lives of children, particularly in their relationships with their primary carers, and continue to have an influence in their later lives.

Example: a mother who experienced great anxiety as a child when her own mother walked away every time she presented challenging or angry behaviour became consistently quiet and compliant as a child and then as an adult. Unconsciously, she identified in her daughter the challenging, angry girl that she herself was unable to be. Over time, the daughter came to view herself, and others saw her, as a challenging, angry person. The characteristics became an integral part of her personality—she identified with her mother's projection of "challenging, angry". Mother and daughter had become involved in recreating the mother's script with her own mother. Mother was then able to identify the projected characteristics in her daughter and overtly oppose and criticize in the daughter the feelings and attitudes that she never explicitly owned or managed in herself. As mother's anxiety about expressing her challenging and angry self had not been worked through, it was repeated (Freud, 1920g; Fraiberg, Adelson, & Shapiro, 1975).

The difference from "projection" alone is that in "projective identification" the recipient of the projected feelings takes them on as his or her own and is then treated by the projector, by him- or herself, and by others as though the feelings, characteristics or behaviour belong to the recipient. The projector can then identify and respond to the feelings in the other and not in him- or herself.

In the example above under Projection, the small child defending his dog has taken in his father's projection of "cross and angry" at that moment and in that situation. If there is a continuation of this projection by the father of his cross and angry feelings into his son, and the son identifies with the projection, projective identification has occurred. The son comes to view himself, and is seen by others, generally as a cross and angry person. Indeed, as he grows up, "cross and angry" becomes a recognized aspect of his personality and of the way in which he and others view him and others relate to him. The sleeping dog is no longer needed as a conduit. This frees father to continue as the strong and coping member of the family with no acknowledgement by anyone of the stress attendant upon that responsible and inflexible role. The father can then identify his projected difficult feelings in his son and attack them there. This protects the status quo, albeit at a significant cost to the child and, indeed, the family.

Why might this situation become problematic? Why does father not own his cross and angry bits? Why might this situation be resistant to change?

The situation may become problematic if the projected-into child finds the stress of being the scapegoat for all family difficulties intolerable and becomes ill. Or the child might become excessively cross and angry outside the family home, such as at school, where he gets into trouble. Or the child might crave the love and affection he does not receive from parents who see him always as cross and angry, and he might begin to steal.

One can speculate that father does not own his cross and angry bits quite simply because if father became regularly cross and angry in response to the demands of his stressful role as good provider for his family, this could have implications and threaten his ability to continue to manage this role. It could also have an impact on his marriage, into which he would take his stresses, which could be understood implicitly as a sign of weakness, according to this family's beliefs about roles and stereotypes. This could impose stress on, and even pose a threat to, the marriage. It is easier and much safer and more acceptable to complain about and struggle with a cross and angry little boy, than to face a stressed and irritable father and a quarrelsome marriage.

Families may also project unmanageable fears or anxieties into a specific individual who then becomes excessively frightening and to be avoided. (See Chapter Nine.) Feelings may also be projected into the world outside, which could lead a child to school refusal. (See Chapter Six, "Thomas".)

Therapists frequently work with families and family members who have suffered from, for example, unmanageable separations, loss, or distress, and who seek refuge in defensive escape as the only apparent solution to their unbearable feelings. Unfortunately, sometimes professionals also find it impossible to stay and struggle with families' seemingly unbearable situations.

> Some of what is so overwhelming . . . is due to unconscious projective mechanisms . . . social workers could be substantially helped to stay with the most traumatised clients, those most prone to flight of various kinds, if there was more provision for them of analytically informed supervision which could help them disengage themselves from what is being projected into them by clients unconsciously disabled by feelings of failure, worthlessness and blame, which they all too easily elicit in their workers, in turn disabling them . . . it cannot be too much stressed that the unconscious does not cease to operate simply because we decide we are not equipped to interpret it. [Temperley, 1979, p. 16]

Overwhelming feelings may be experienced by clinical therapists as well as community workers in their work with families.

Without an understanding of the mechanism of "projective identification", therapists may identify with these projected unmanageable feelings and become overwhelmed and confused, possibly leading to an unfortunate repetition by professionals of the rejections, separations, and losses that the families have suffered and by which they have been previously distressed and even traumatized. Also, therapists' own personal issues can be triggered by, or projected into, the families' material and, if feelings are unrecognized and seem unmanageable, can present obstacles in the therapy. For example, a therapist's unresolved experience of loss and helplessness as a child, through abandonment or bereavement, may become triggered by the family's struggle with a contemporary loss and feeling of helplessness.

Displacement

An understanding of displacement can also provide useful information about a child's emotional life. In play, a child may redirect dangerous or unacceptable feelings, such as unexpressed and maybe unacknowledged anger or jealousy felt towards a newborn sibling. These dangerous feelings will be vented on a safer object, such as a doll, which may be poked and torn apart. The child will experience the feelings safely and only in relation to the doll, who is reported as having been "naughty". In this way, strong and frightening feelings are expressed and communicated, and, indeed, released, in a harmless way on to an inanimate object. If the play is understood, the child is likely to feel relief and no one has been harmed.

In a similar way, a mother may displace frightening emotion felt towards an adult family member, maybe a partner, on to a child. The mother may feel resentful and frustrated towards her partner. She is afraid that the partner will leave her if she expresses her feelings towards him, and so she begins to become resentful, frustrated, and constantly critical towards her child, whom she knows cannot leave. The child is again a more available and apparently "safer" target for these difficult and scary feelings, though this process would clearly distort the parent–child relationship. Most worryingly, this is clearly dangerous and damaging for the child. An astute and well-informed therapist working with the family would be able to identify the process of displacement. This could lead to work with the couple towards more open and trusting communication.

In other situations, anxiety originating in a child's relationship with his or her family may be displaced on to school or school teachers, so that a school phobia develops. The displacement protects the child from experiencing directly hostile or anxious feelings towards parents, who are important and indispensable to a young child. The feelings are displaced on to school and the child attempts to avoid the anxiety by avoiding school. It is clearly of importance that professionals are aware of this possibility of displaced feelings as a defence in assessing a child with school phobia, in order to decide whether the intervention should be best directed with the school, the family, or with the child him- or herself.

"Displacement" is different to "projection". In "displacement", the individual owns and bears the feeling, but experiences and expresses it, for example, in relation to the doll instead of towards the baby. On the other hand, in "projection", the child projects into (i.e., arouses in) another person (perhaps an older sibling) his or her anger and jealousy that may actually be felt towards the baby. The sibling then experiences these feelings. There are also similarities and overlaps between these two processes.

Splitting

> To hate the one you love, because you are frustrated, can be a cata-
> strophically frightening feeling, when you are so dependent; to love
> the one you hate, exceedingly difficult when explosive fits of rage
> have taken over the whole of experience for the time being. [Jaques,
> 1968, p. 36]

A young infant may initially manage the challenge of experiencing strong conflicting feelings by "splitting" the feelings. So, when the loving and hating feelings are experienced towards the same person, particularly when that person is a parent and it does not feel safe to experience and express both emotions to the one parent, the child may manage the conflict by the defence of "splitting" the good and the bad parts. The child would then attempt to keep the parts separate and directed towards different "objects" or people. In this way, he or she experiences and expresses all the "good" loving feelings towards one person and all "bad" aggressive feelings towards another: for example, two parents. Now, for the child, some people are all good and others all bad and the recipient of strong negative feelings, such as anger and hatred. The split makes the feelings more manageable for the child. (See also Chapter One, "Melanie Klein".)

Splitting as a way of dealing with difficulties and confused or conflicting feelings is a well-developed method used by children, and also by adults. It makes the feelings of love and hate more manageable. While growing up, the child needs enough of his or her own good experiences of being loved and of emotions being held and thought about, so that bad experiences can be managed and integrated (Bion, 1962, 1967). The child is then better able to resolve internal splits and acknowledge angry and hating, as well as loving, feelings for one person without fear that that person will be destroyed. For example: "I love you, mum, but I hate it when you . . ."; or else: "I hate you when . . .", and the loving part is understood by both.

In the course of this resolution, the child may move between splitting when the feelings are too difficult and integration when this is manageable. Failure in time to accomplish integration of feelings can lead to difficulties and dysfunction in later life.

Everyday examples of a child attempting to split his or her parents are very familiar. For example, if mum says, "no, you can't have a chocolate now," in the child's mind she becomes the mean, withholding parent and the child may feel it is worth trying dad for a different, more acceptable answer. If dad does agree to the chocolate, he then becomes the good parent for the child in this situation. In order to make the split effective and the feelings kept apart, the child is reliant upon the adults not consulting with each other or presenting a united front. The child may take advantage of a situation where parents actively, or deliberately, undermine each other.

As these conflicts and splits occur and may cause dysfunction or illness within the individual, so also they can occur within families—between individual family members and between dyads or groups of individuals within families. In this way, certain individuals, pairings or groups may be seen as the good one(s) in the family and other individuals or groups as the bad and problematic members. So, one child or parent is seen as the "bad" one and another as "good". (See Chapters Six, Seven, and Nine.)

Within a reliable and containing relationship within the therapy room, the therapist works with family members to identify and reintegrate parts split off into each other and invites the safe expression of unacknowledged or conflictual feelings. For example, where an adolescent is referred with depression, family members can be helped to own, articulate, and manage their own more depressive aspects and the adolescent supported to take back some hopefulness which the family had located only in others. Children and adults are supported to find a way of recognizing the "good" and "bad" in the same person, so that, for example, they are able to recognize the positive as well as the more difficult aspects of both parents. (See Chapter Nine.)

Therapy supports parents in being able to work together as a united couple, making joint decisions either in agreement or refusal. They work at thinking about emotional issues and experiences together, making connections between thoughts, behaviour, and feelings, so that the child feels contained. The parental couple avoids creating confusion about family norms and are clear in their joint decisions. In this way, they can provide a reliable shared structure for family life with rules and expectations which they promote and enforce together. Through the experience of a containing reliable structure provided by parents, the child can learn to manage both good and bad feelings and to cope with conflict and life's frustrations and disappointments.

Hence, it is considered of great importance that in two-parent families both parents attend family sessions. This makes clear that there is no acceptance of, or collusion with, any possible devaluation or marginalization of any family member. Where parents are no longer together, and particularly where there is continuing conflict and even animosity between the parents, the composition of conjoint family meetings would need to be carefully considered and planned with the families. Children should not be subjected in the therapy room to being drawn excessively into their parents' fights or conflict, or attempts at splits into "good" and "bad". However, children may be greatly helped by parents who are able to show them that, while they are no longer a couple, they can still meet and think together as parents in the interests of the children.

These differing perceptions of good and bad occur both within the family and by outside professionals and agencies. The child also benefits if all involved, such as teachers and therapists together with their parents, share and uphold a common idea of expected and acceptable behaviour. Disagreement by others to parents' limits makes the limits seem harsher and less reasonable. Hostile and aggressive parental enforcement of rules can evoke antipathy and aggressive response by children to those rules. Support and respect for parents by professionals, together with help for parents, where necessary, to uphold rules in a firm, thoughtful, and non-threatening manner, helps children to manage and internalize limits.

Professionals, including therapists, can become involved in splits. A therapist may come to feel completely bad and useless in work with certain children or families who may idealize other adults, such as family members and current or previous professionals. A child living away from home, either in an alternative home or in a hospital, can develop a conflict of loyalty and affection between birth and other home. The child may feel some guilt and confusion at liking the alternative carers, such as hospital staff or foster carers, whom they may find less strict and more fun than their own parents. The child may try to manage this confusion of emotions by splitting and keeping separate the feelings of love and hate, the positive and negative. The hospital staff or foster home may become all good and the birth home all bad, or vice versa.

At the end of work with one therapist, families can experience a sense of loss and mourning. If they move to a new therapist, a task may be to understand a family's hostility towards the new therapist as a way of avoiding difficult and conflicting feelings about the loss. This may relate to a good experience with the previous therapist and also to a previous negative experience, which can also involve mourning and regret that it was not better. The therapist can name and acknowledge some of these expectable responses so that it is acceptable that change involves loss and often difficult and conflicting feelings. Ambivalence or idealization towards the current therapist may also have emanated from the family's perception of all difficulties as belonging in the past, for example, with a previous therapist, or in the outside world. The therapist will invite the expression of conflictual feelings in the reliable therapy space so that they can be shared, expressed, and thought about. In this way, the families can feel stronger to manage a range of feelings and have less need for defences against them.

Identification with the aggressor

Application of psychoanalytic theory can offer some explanation for apparently puzzling repeated behaviour where similar psychological or emotional difficulties and distress are transmitted from one generation to the next.

Why, for example, would parents who have themselves suffered abuse, neglect, and abandonment in their own childhood seem to repeat their past in the present with their own children?

This intergenerational repetition of social and emotional psychopathology may be understood in psychoanalytic terms as a form of defence known as "identification with the aggressor": an individual allies with the enemy for protection, as this seems to be safer. The individual then becomes like the aggressor but does not know how this happened, as the process is unconscious.

This form of defence can also be used therapeutically with children to work out feelings, either against or in co-operation with the therapist. Anna Freud (1936) pointed out "that there are many children's games in which through the metamorphosis of the subject into a dreaded object anxiety is converted into pleasurable security" (p. 119). By becoming the roaring tiger in a game, the child identifies with the feared object, and when he or she is the tiger, then there is no need to fear the tiger. The first stage for the therapist is to recognize the feeling (e.g., fear) and name it as existing in the room, before it is identified in an individual. By recognizing the child's defence, the therapist gains insight into the true nature of the feeling communicated.

So, children who are hospitalized may be subjected to unpleasant and painful medical procedures over which they have no control and in which their parents are experienced as being complicit. In play, a child may identify with the hurting nurse or doctor as the aggressor, and in the game become the attacking and powerful person who "injects" and "operates on" the therapist. Hospital play specialists and therapists have many such experiences of playing patient and being "subjected to" unpleasant procedures. "And now you know what it is like," the child might be thinking, as the pretend needle hits the therapist's arm. Through an understanding of children's use of this defence, therapists can, either directly with the child or with the family, provide a containing space and presence for working on the fear and pain of these frightening procedures.

> Play enables the child to master the disturbing event or situation by actively bringing it about, rather than being the passive and helpless spectator. Playing to master disturbing events is still an explanation in terms of striving for pleasure and escape from pain, since the repetition is held to reduce the unpleasant disturbance. [Millar, 1972, p. 29]

The identification is dependent upon an individual taking in some quality of another person, for example power, control, ability to hurt/be frightening. (See Chapter Seven.) This defence may be used where the emotional responses to the feared or painful experience or procedure have not yet been safely contained.

Nature and appearance of unconscious processes, including transference and countertransference, the Oedipal stage, and free association

An individual's or family's unconscious feelings, wishes, fears, and anxieties can be recognized by the therapist through processes such as transference and countertransference. Therapy with families does not attempt actively to bring the less accessible parts of individuals' unconscious material to consciousness. Nevertheless, a good working knowledge of the unconscious and its processes can be important for therapists working with families: its nature and the ways in which it plays a part in a person's mental and emotional life and behaviour; how it may operate within families and between individuals; its linking of the past with the present; and how it may irrationally obstruct or impede progress towards change.

The unconscious is sometimes portrayed as containing wild destructive forces, which the ego (the developed self) is struggling to control. If feelings are held in check because of the belief that they may be dangerous, misunderstood, and unmanageable, they are more likely to be acted out in continuing destructive or difficult behaviour. Therapists may feel understandable apprehension at times about allowing children and families to express themselves too freely in therapy in case they feel swamped and unable to cope. On the other hand, therapists also recognize that families can work towards a true expression of feelings and worries with someone they trust and who can promote understanding. This is a way to make sense of feelings and to move on in constructive ways.

While family therapists do not interpret the transference and countertransference, knowledge of these phenomena as they may occur in therapy with families can be illuminating and helpful to the therapists and thus of notable assistance to the families with whom they meet. While a family therapist may not, and indeed should not, interpret the transference and their own countertransference in their work with families, they may benefit from being alert and sensitive to these processes, which can then contribute to the therapy.

Transference

The theoretical understanding of the process of the transference in clinical practice was first formulated and written up by Sigmund Freud. Whether or not we are consciously aware of it, transference occurs in all our relationships and interactions with other people, as we bring to present encounters aspects of previous involvement with others in the past.

The general formalized theory of the transference, dating from Sigmund Freud, was that the patient transfers on to the analyst feelings and fantasies from primary relationships with parents. Eventually, the neurotic conflict which has endured and evolved in relationships with parents manifests itself in the transference relationship with the analyst. So, a patient who experienced fear in relation to a parent unknowingly transfers that earlier relationship to the present one with the therapist, in which the patient becomes fearful and views the therapist as frightening. Klein maintained that even in very small, dependent children the development of the transference can occur.

In *Fragment of an Analysis of a Case of Hysteria* ("Dora"), Freud defined the transference as a

... special class of mental structures, for the most part unconscious ... [these are] new editions or facsimiles of the impulses or fantasies which are aroused and made conscious during the process of analysis; but they have this peculiarity, which is characteristic for their species, that they replace some earlier person by the person of the physician. [Freud, 1905e, p. 116]

Through the analyst becoming the new object or recipient of the patient's old, unresolved conflicts, the process of better understanding and unravelling the past and its current impact are facilitated.

This unconscious repetition, in which present relationships are unconsciously attributed qualities of internalized figures and relationships from the past, is an occurrence evoked not only in the analytic setting, though this clinical situation is specifically designed to enhance it. It is present also in everyday life and demonstrated most clearly in situations of unmanageable stress, anxiety, or emotional conflict (Fraiberg, 1978, p. 88).

Family therapists frequently meet with families, and particularly with children, who are in a state of severe emotional conflict and distress. Old ghosts and internalized figures from the past are regularly brought into the therapy room, either explicitly or, more often, by inference. The ability or not of the therapist to make an effective relationship with the family and to begin to uncover with them a different understanding of their difficulties may be enhanced by this knowledge from psychoanalysis.

For example: a girl whose childhood experience of a frightening father might lead her to grow up with an internalized model of herself in relationship to men who will always frighten or hurt her; or a boy, brought up by a rejecting and neglectful mother might grow up viewing himself in relationship only with uncaring women who will be the same and he will find evidence to confirm his belief. Or a baby who repeatedly experienced his mother as frightened and rejecting whenever he became angry might grow up with the constant concern that his angry feelings are dangerous and threatening to love and security. In family meetings this may be recognized in a parent who withdraws when emotions become heated, causing the whole family to avoid "scenes" and never resolve difficult issues. In this way, the parent is allowed to control an uneasy peace because of anxieties from many years ago. By acknowledging that angry feelings may continue to be scary but can be safely explored within the secure therapy setting, a therapist can support the family towards more open emotional communication.

Alternatively, the transference may be on to therapists, who are perceived as scary, not understanding or caring, being hurtful or unreliable, and about to walk away. The transference may include hostility and mistrust and even rejection of the therapist. The origins of the transferred feelings and hurt can be understood and explored by the therapist together with the family. Failure to recognize and understand this process might lead to the therapist feeling overwhelmed by the transferred feelings and unable to continue in the therapy. Importantly, also, an unconscious transference on to the present relationship with the therapist of an internalized experience of neglect or rejection in the past can be triggered by the therapist's actual absence, lateness, or other signs of unreliability.

Therapists with families may be divided about the way in which this transference of feelings should be handled. To avoid the feelings and concentrate only on present objective reality is to ignore a powerful communication by the family and to miss the opportunity of using this information in a constructive way. On the other hand, to interpret the feelings which seem to be impeding the progress of the therapy could be considered to be outside the brief and capability of the family therapist. A third possibility is that the therapist understands the family's transference of feelings and openly communicates this to the family.

For example:

- therapist is feeling provoked and tested in family meetings by a mother;
- therapist recognizes that the mother is being quarrelsome in the way she reported that she used to be in the past with her own mother who subsequently abandoned her. The therapist notes this but does not interpret it in relation to the mother's own experience. Instead, she links it to the young woman's current problematic relationship with her small daughter, who has been referred with oppositional behaviour. The therapist needs to understand and manage the transfer of feelings by the

mother so that she does not also in turn act out against her and maybe abandon the therapy;

- the therapist observes to the mother that she is finding her child troublesome in the way she described herself with her own mother. Importantly, the therapist uses the mother's own report of her earlier relationship. The mother's unexpressed fear of abandonment in the therapy can then be productively acknowledged. Additionally, she can be congratulated on struggling with her difficulties and trying to provide for her daughter a different experience from her own rejection as a child.

In family meetings, it can be important and relevant to relate the current transfer of feelings back to the original relationships, feelings, and experience in the life of the family or family members. This serves not to criticize or to pathologize, but simply to illuminate.

For example, a therapist might observe in a straightforward way that she experiences the whole family's, or a single family member's, reactions to her as replicating what they have reported of a relationship with a significant figure in the past (e.g., great reverence or, conversely, total contempt for a grandmother). It would be inappropriate for the therapist to make direct transference interpretations. However, in this way, she may usefully provide the family with an increased awareness of the true nature and acknowledged origin of the transferred feelings in order to further the family's self-understanding as a way of moving towards change (Winnicott, 1970).

The reaction to a therapist by a family member or the family as a whole is also likely to be influenced by unconscious factors, such as resemblance of the therapist, or not, to others in the past, whom the family may or may not have liked. The unconscious may reveal itself through a tone of voice or gesture, or through an impulsive action or expression of emotion that may communicate underlying and unspoken feelings. Whether or not transference reactions are clearly obvious, they are present and are affected by the therapist's own behaviour and attitude. The therapist's reactions to family members and to the family as a whole are similarly influenced by the therapist's own internal figures from earlier experiences and relationships. For example, the therapist may have an instinctive and unconscious deferential reaction to older males as being wise and always correct, emanating from an internalized model of the therapist with his or her own father who was experienced as unquestionable and intellectually superior.

Patrick Casement has written particularly helpfully on what happens between analyst and patient in the analytic space and process and on the potential for analysts/therapists learning from their patients (Casement, 1985, 1990).

Psychoanalysis tends to be associated with the analysis of symptoms, dreams, and free-associated slips of the tongue, "Freudian slips", and with the containment, consideration, and resolution of conflicting unmanageable feelings. Equal and important attention is also paid to what is transferred on to the analyst and to the analyst's reaction evoked in response—the analyst's countertransference experience.

Countertransference

The countertransference may be viewed as a mirror image of the transference. As the analyst monitors and seeks to understand his or her own reaction to the patient, so therapists can also use their own experience and responses with families as important information about the family, their emotional life, relationships, and losses. In addition to what family members say and how they relate to each other, clues to a family's difficulties may lie also in what the therapist feels with the family in the therapy room. Therapists cannot avoid or escape the feelings, which can be powerful, but they can be helped to make sense of overwhelming emotions aroused in them in the course of family sessions. At times, it may be difficult and alarming to acknowledge the strength of the angry, useless, helpless feelings experienced by therapists. An understanding that the family's unbearable feelings in present relationships in the room may have been triggered by internalized relationships from the past would support the therapist in managing countertransference feelings of, for example, anxiety, hopelessness, or anger. This information may be crucial for the continuation of a challenging therapy task.

A family therapist may be alerted to his or her countertransference reaction by experiencing a deviation from usual practice of "neutrality", also called "even-handedness", or "involved impartiality" (Stierlin, 1977, p. 313). The therapist may become aware of this deviation through seeming to "take sides", or being more interested in certain family members, or having specific thoughts or feelings towards individuals. The therapist's maintenance of a "meta-position" is essential in enabling him or her to experience and respond compassionately to the feelings of the family while keeping a reflective, thoughtful presence. Knowledge of the countertransference may help to prevent therapists from over-identifying or becoming inappropriately drawn into family life. (See "Process"—"Formation of relationships between therapist and family", above.)

Therapists may be repeatedly stirred up by the process of therapy, where they are involved with families in considering and struggling with emotionally highly-charged situations and difficulties. Relationships within the family can frequently be fraught and sometimes close to breaking point. Aspects of the therapist's own life, relationships, and difficulties may be transferred into the work with the families and this could be mistaken for countertransference. This needs to be clearly understood by the therapist so that his or her own personal issues or assumptions about family life do not intrude into the work. Only through their own equivalent of a psychoanalytic training analysis would a family therapist be truly equipped to distinguish his or her own unresolved personal material from countertransference information emanating from the family and which can be beneficially used in the therapy.

The feelings in the countertransference can be so intense that, unless the feelings are recognized and acknowledged, therapists may even act them out by being late, blaming parents or colleagues when there is no progress, requesting work transfers, or even leaving feeling "burned out". The therapist also needs to be able to distinguish between countertransference feelings aroused by the transference from the family or family member and the therapist's own feelings in relation to the therapy, to the family, or to the subject of discussion.

In work with families, the therapist may be aware of being drawn into taking a specific role in a family or feeling an urge to do so: for example, feeling infantilized and playing an absent child, or feeling revered with an impulse uncharacteristically to dispense wise advice, as a grandparent might. If carefully monitored, these feelings and urges may give important information about what is missing for the family, where the gaps are for them, what the losses may have been (e.g., a missing child or deceased grandparent).

For example, a therapist notices that a usually competent family is struggling to make plans for a holiday. The struggle seems out of proportion to the task and is distressing for the mother and youngest child who is in tears and cannot understand. The mother delegates the task to the children who become more distressed and frustrated and say they do not know and they want their usual holiday. The parents cannot make a decision. The therapist is having great difficulty not intervening and offering clear choices and advice, something that she would never usually do or think of doing. She reflects on this.

Family therapist: "This decision seems so difficult for you. I wonder if your mother [directed at mother of family] was usually involved in organizing family holidays with you. This is your first summer since her death and perhaps it is difficult to think about the holiday without her."

The family is quiet and the mother nods. The conversation is freed and the parents say that they will make plans for the holiday that evening, which the therapist learns the following week that they have done, choosing the usual family holiday, even without grandmother this year. The therapist's own experience with the family can give crucial information on the real nature of this distress and difficulty for them.

Oedipal stage

From his investigations into dreams, Sigmund Freud offered his idea that a dream in which a loved person dies may often indicate an unconscious wish for the death of that person. To understand this idea further, Freud turned to the emotional life of children. He hypothesized that in early childhood it was the norm and not the exception for young children to experience negative feelings such as hatred and anger, as well as loving feelings, towards their parents and siblings. In this way, Freud formed and introduced his ideas about what he called oedipal jealousy or rivalry and the Oedipus complex (Freud, 1900a).

The theory of the Oedipus complex maintains that, universally in the course of healthy psychological development, young children between the ages of four and six years experience an unconscious desire for an exclusive relationship with the parent of the opposite sex. This wish requires possession of the desired parent in competition with the other parent, resulting in an anxiety-ridden rivalry with the same-sex parent. This stage of development is resolved only when the child has successfully identified with the parent of the same sex.

Freud, in the late nineteenth and first half of the twentieth centuries, made an assumption about a male–female parenting couple which would not be made in some parts of the world in the early twenty-first century. However, his presentation and understanding of the Oedipus complex and its resolution can be adapted to the greater variety in contemporary family composition.

So, at this stage, and following increasing awareness by the growing infant of the mother as a separate person, the young child comes to realize that there is another person closely connected to the mother: the child's father/mother's partner. (See Chapter One, "Donald Winnicott"). For all concerned, this transition from a two-person to a three-person relationship is challenging, and the child, according to Freud, manages in this specific way. The child has not yet developed the capacity to bear a sense of isolation and exclusion from the parental couple, to relate to the couple as a unit as well as two separate people, and to recognize the generational boundary between him- or herself and this exclusive twosome. It is also challenging for the parental couple at this time to continue to maintain and enjoy their separateness and freedom as a two-person relationship, while also becoming a threesome. The child has also not yet managed the integration of feelings of love and hostility towards the same parent, so splits all loving feelings for one parent (who is desired) and all hostility towards the other (of whom the child wishes to be rid). In this way, the conflicting feelings can be borne. Until these developmental tasks are mastered, the child seeks to separate off the individual parents in order to take the place of the same sex parent and form a couple with the other parent. (See "Family examples" below.)

Free association

Freud introduced the technique of free association by asking patients to speak of whatever came into their minds, however trivial or embarrassing this seemed and even though the most painful memories may be beyond conscious recall. In practice with families, the therapist would have no formula or planned agenda for meetings, but would invite and follow what the family brought, which was most pressing for them. (See Chapter Five, "Clara".) If, for example, the family did not speak about the most obvious subject, such as eating when a child has an eating disorder, the therapist might be curious about why this was. The therapist also makes connections between what the family does or does not bring for discussion and the issues with which they want help to make changes.

Importance of interpretation and containment

Interpretation, along with transference and countertransference, is a fundamental tool of psychoanalysis and of psychoanalytic psychotherapy.

> This case strengthened my growing conviction that a precondition for the psychoanalysis of a child is to understand and interpret the phantasies, feelings, anxieties and experiences expressed by play or, if play activities are inhibited, the causes of the inhibition. [Klein, 1955, p. 6]

The purpose of the interpretation in child psychoanalysis is to understand and describe to the child the feelings and fantasies that appear to be expressed in the play and in the relationship between child and analyst. By connecting and interpreting at an emotional level, the analyst's aim is to give relief and reassurance to the patient through verbal acknowledgement of what has been unspeakable and of feelings that have felt instinctively too dangerous to be allowed overt expression. This process then allows change to occur. Klein observed in her work that this seemed to bring relief to the child: "The effect of this interpretation on the child was striking: her anxiety and distrust first increased, but very soon gave way to obvious relief" (*ibid.*, p. 7).

Through the analyst's interpretation, the child is shown that the underlying meaning of the play has been recognized and accepted. In this way, the child's play becomes a form of communication between child and analyst, not simply an individual repeated activity for the child alone. Also, in this way, the child can be freed from expending energy on repressing unwanted feelings, and the play and the communication may then become freer and more relaxed and enjoyable.

While therapists working with families would not make interpretations of the unconscious, they do offer a different understanding of the underlying or unspoken nature of difficulties which families face in order to bring insight and relief. For example, a young person who steals might really want a parent's time, not money; a young person refusing to do rehabilitation exercises might fear losing "parents-together time" if she is well. This different understanding of difficulties can be tested by the families and either developed or modified, depending on response and on new information that becomes available.

For example, a therapist discusses with a family a teenager's stealing. The therapist offers an understanding that the behaviour may indicate an unspoken and unrecognized problem to which the young person is drawing parents' attention. The family can then consider the behaviour differently and explore other possible meanings and solutions.

For example, a therapist wonders why a teenage girl with somatoform disorder would fail to do rehabilitation exercises. The girl does not know. The therapist understands that continuing immobility brings together her (divorced) parents for hospital appointments, the only time that she sees them together. The girl says nothing more. The therapist asks the parents at what other time they might be together with their daughter, and they plan to think about this.

Some therapists with families at times include in family meetings a "reflecting team". The team are separate from the therapy conversation, in which they do not take part, but they do comment on the conversation in specific interludes for this purpose. Alternatively, a therapist or co-therapists with families might incorporate in the room both components of conversation and reflection: in this model, the therapist(s) themselves would alternate between engaging in the conversation and stepping back to offer thoughts or reflections.

This may relate to the process of interpretation that involves the uncovering and attribution of new meaning to previously uncommunicated elements in relationships or experiences. In a therapy relationship with families, this process may be used to gain a new and different understanding of a presenting problem.

An understanding or interpretation of the therapist's countertransference (i.e., the therapist's experience in relationship with the family in the therapy room) may be thought silently in the therapist's head and used in this way to aid reflection on what the family have brought to the therapy. The importance for the therapist is to understand the transference, but not necessarily to voice the understanding explicitly in the therapy room (Magagna, 2005, p. 187). The therapist's understanding might relate to the family's anger about a break in therapy, distress at loss of a previous therapist, jealousy of other family member's use of therapy time, content at therapist's reliability and predictability.

Subsequently, the concept of "containment" was developed particularly by Bion (1962, 1967), building on the work of Klein and the object relations school on the importance of a "holding other" in the development of the young infant. It refers not only to the essential presence of the other (e.g., the child's parent), but also to the communicated capacity of the other to bear, understand, and process feelings which seem to the child at that moment to be overwhelming and out of control. In this way, the infant experiences safe emotional holding, or containment.

Similarly, in therapy settings, the holding mental stance of the therapist together with a secure, reliable environment provides a predictable thinking space for the family. Within this setting it will become safe for family members to own, acknowledge and express difficult different feelings in their relationships with each other, for example dislike, hatred and aggression, as well as love. (See "Family examples", Chapters Four to Nine.)

Affect regulation, emotional communication, and "mentalization"

Following on the writings of the early psychoanalysts, more recent thinking has developed on the process of individuals being able to think about, understand, and respond to feelings and behaviour in themselves and others and particularly within significant relationships. This process, akin to "theory of mind", has become known as the "mentalization" of emotional experience, or the capacity to think about the experience of oneself and others within the relationship and to give it symbols (or words): the representation of "feelings, wishes, beliefs and desires in an attachment context (mentalization)" (Fonagy, 2005). "This process of mentalization (Fonagy, 2004) consists of the identification and then naming of the experience and thus symbolizing it (Segal, 1957), so that the name can be recalled and applied to the feeling state when it recurs" (Bakalar, 2005). An important aspect of mentalization is the recognition of alternatives. So, a child, for example, would come to recognize that in his or her relationship with a parent, the feelings and behaviour of both child and parent were not inevitable and had alternative possibilities.

Allan Schore recognized the importance of the young child's primary attachment relationship to the child's future ability to regulate his or her own emotions. Schore connected the influence of this relationship on aspects of the child's brain development necessary for affect regulation, recognition of emotions in self and others, and the management of stress (Schore, 1994).

The therapy setting provides families with a safe space in which to find a language to describe their own and others' feelings and to develop emotional communication. In this way, emotions that have felt too difficult, frightening, or embarrassing to bear or acknowledge can be explored and, in time, owned, recognized, and talked about.

Example: A boy of nine years old experiences the sudden death of a much loved grandparent. He is overwhelmed by great sadness. He feels tearful and has some physical and emotional sensations evocative of earlier times when he had temper tantrums. The cross feelings are familiar to him but he is unable to identify or name the new sad feeling. His mother has become withdrawn in reaction to the loss and his father is working away for some time. He has no parent available to help him understand his sad feeling and he begins to behave as he did earlier when he was cross—he has tantrums. This draws in his mother's attention, and his father's when he returns home, and they seek professional help because they cannot understand or cope with the boy's anger. The whole family see a therapist, who invites a conversation about their loss and feelings, and they all come to understand that the whole family, including the boy, is sad. The boy now has a symbol to describe his new feeling, "sadness", which he can identify in future and distinguish this feeling from anger.

An important aspect of this process is that within the safe setting, feelings can be experienced as more bearable and talking possible. They can be managed both by the individual and within relationships, with the support of other family members. (See "Family examples", below).

Summary

So, psychoanalytic theory can offer to therapy with families ideas about present difficulties in the context of current family relationships which are linked to unresolved relationships in the past; recognition by therapists of different dilemmas and challenges for individual family members which may relate to past events and relationships; connections made jointly by therapists and families together between current difficulties and past unresolved issues; observable behaviour and styles of relating being not always totally rational and transparent but being affected by processes of which individuals may not be immediately consciously aware; apparent resistance and reluctance to change being a manifestation of individuals' and families' defences which have been organized to offer necessary protection and which need to be respected, understood, and worked with carefully; individuals struggling with ambivalence and conflicting thoughts and feelings which can be articulated and reflected upon when they feel safely contained.

The challenges for therapists are many, and include therapists finding and developing their own individual stance and style within which they can engage and form a therapeutic relationship with family members and with the family as a unit; providing safe containment within therapy meetings so that families can move on to speak about what seemed previously unbearable; and supporting family members in the development of emotional communication and the search for their own solutions. Therapists are also challenged with making helpful connections between painful and unresolved feelings and events from the past as they are triggered by conflicts and difficulties in present relationships. Individuals may experience internal conflicts of feelings that, if not resolved internally, can intrude into the current family situation and relationships.

For example: a mother who loves her own mother, but all through her childhood was greatly distressed by feelings of anger and hatred at her mother's control of her, resists the most straightforward requests by her own adolescent daughter as they feel like further attempts at control; the daughter experiences her mother as rejecting and unavailable to her and becomes ill; they attend for therapy and in time discuss this important issue between them.

In the following chapters, a number of different child and family mental health presentations is discussed, to each of which similar principles and concepts are applied. In practice with families, the principles which owe their origin to psychoanalytic thinking and theory include: the development of a therapeutic relationship within which change can occur, with therapist working alongside the family demonstrating interest in and understanding of their struggles and conflicts; provision by therapists of space for individual family members, as indicated, where they may further explore and understand their own internal issues and how these relate to current family difficulties; acknowledgement by therapists of ambivalence and conflict and the function of defences which protect against what has previously felt unbearable; families internalizing from their therapy meetings and developing the capacity to think about their issues; the experience of therapists in the therapy and how this might help further understanding of the families' difficulties.

CHAPTER FOUR

Young children with feeding difficulties

P arental concern about the feeding of infants and young children is not unusual. Over 50% of parents of babies and children between nine months and seven years report concerns about feeding behaviour and over 20% report a number of difficulties (Crist & Napier-Phillips, 2001). Most of the difficulties resolve over time or with the help and intervention of a primary healthcare professional.

It is, of course, not known how many other parents may, at times, have worries about feeding in the early days and months of a child's life but do not get to the point of seeking professional advice. Feeding is crucial and central to a child's ability not only to grow and flourish, but, indeed, to survive. Concerns by parents in this vital area of care are, therefore, neither surprising nor remarkable.

> Studies investigating the prevalence rates of eating problems in normal British children have found that one-third of children by the age of five years have had mild to moderate eating difficulties. Of this group, two-thirds suffer from faddy eating and the rest do not eat enough. Eating problems were also found to be more prevalent

in low birth-weight babies but less prevalent in large families. [Fox & Joughin, 2002, p. 8]

Criteria for specific diagnosis of a feeding disorder include feeding disturbance manifested by persistent failure to eat adequately with significant failure to gain weight or significant loss of weight over at least one month; disturbance is not due to associated gastrointestinal or other medical condition, for example, oesophageal reflux; disturbance is not better accounted for by another mental health disorder, for example, rumination disorder, or by lack of available food; onset is before age six years.

Some persistent feeding disorders do fit into the diagnostic category, but many do not, as causes are complicated and the difficulty maintained by a number of different factors. The difficulties that reach tiers two and three of the child and family consultation services are often complex and may comprise a mixture of medical, psychological, and social factors. Sometimes, there is a cultural component also. When babies or young children, with or without any medical problems, are referred with feeding difficulties to a mental health service, the feeding relationship is the focus of change. It is less usual for an older child or adolescent to be referred, though this does occur.

Psychoanalytic perspective

A psychoanalytical understanding of feeding difficulties early in an infant's life is based on thinking of the mother–infant relationship as underpinning and being central to the development of effective feeding. Conversely, the developing feeding relationship contributes to and enhances the mother–infant bond.

Additionally, a psychoanalytic view would assume the incorporation into the development of the mother–infant feeding relationship of the mother's own experience of having her feeding and emotional needs met, both currently and, importantly, in her own infancy and childhood.

> I have argued that parental deprivation, unmediated by past or current supportive relationships, has a central part to play in the development of feeding difficulties in infancy. However, it is

important within the parent–infant configuration to take into account the particular qualities the infant brings to the development of such difficulties or, alternatively, a capacity to overcome these difficulties. By this I mean that there is always a "fit" between a mother and her infant. The degree of "fit" depends not only on the mother's capacity in general, but also her particular capacity to deal with and respond to the constellation of feelings that are aroused in her by the baby. Some infants arouse in the mother a sense of her ability to understand and meet the needs of a particular baby. Feeding, at a physical and emotional level, is experienced as rewarding. On the other hand, some infants seem to push the mother beyond her own limitations or to arouse in her emotional experiences which are difficult for her. [Driggs, 2000, p. 68]

The infant brings to the feeding relationship aspects of him- or herself that fit and resonate with the mother's contribution from experience. Alternately, what the infant brings may grate or fit uncomfortably with the mother, and this ill-fit can lead to difficulties and distress.

The development of feeding between mother and infant is also importantly about the regulation of closeness and distance in the parent–child relationship. As Daws (1997) writes, it is not to say that close is good and distant is bad, but that through the medium of feeding the relationship is regulated so that, hopefully, an appropriate fit is found between mother and baby. However, this fit does not always comfortably occur.

A psychoanalytic approach and understanding also acknowledge the possibility of ambivalence in the mother, which may not be overt and clearly recognized, since the mother may feel that any doubts and conflictual feelings about her new role as parent are not acceptable either to herself or to others.

There may be conscious or unconscious memories from the mother's own past experience, or else current difficulties or depression, which can affect the mother–child relationship at this crucial time as the mother strives to establish regular feeding. Any difficulties, however minor, in establishing regular "good enough" feeding of her baby may, in turn, persecute the mother with ideas that she herself is not a good enough mother, or even that she is a bad one. Consequent feelings of distress, anxiety, and hopelessness may further exacerbate a difficult situation.

Alan Stein's research found a connection between feeding difficulties in children and disturbed eating habits and attitudes in mothers. This work was important in highlighting the need to address the eating habits and attitudes of parents when a child presents with an eating difficulty and to work with the child's primary relationships as well as with the referred behaviour (Stein, Stein, Walters, & Fairburn, 1995).

Additionally, where an infant is sick, disabled, struggling to thrive or even to survive in the neonatal period, parents may need to adjust to overwhelming feelings of loss and grieving for the anticipated and hoped-for perfect, healthy child which currently they do not have. Instead, they spend sleepless, worried nights at the hospital, and are present and participant in unpleasant, invasive investigations of their child. They may be assailed by feelings of failure to produce the perfect, or even good enough, baby that everyone was expecting.

If the infant is in hospital, the parents are unable even to care for, nurture, or protect their child. They contribute to medical procedures, as they choose to hold and restrain their child in order to try to minimize distress and give the child what care, comfort, and protection they can. At other times, they must attempt to remain at a certain distance and refrain from becoming too involved with their own new infant, who seems to belong to professionals who can meet their baby's complicated needs while they, as parents, cannot.

Because of these unfortunate circumstances, parents may also consciously or unconsciously hold back from engaging emotionally with their infant, fearful of investing too completely in a baby whose future is uncertain and whose hold on life itself may, at times, be precarious. On the other hand, such difficult early experiences and traumatic events for both parents and child may lead the parents later in the child's life to worry and protect their child excessively.

During early separations, when care of the sick infant is taken over totally by professionals, the mother may frequently be beset by a maelstrom of feelings of helplessness, hopelessness, and possible preparation for the continuing sickness or even death of her child. It is not difficult to see how the relationship between mother and child may continue to struggle to function optimally in all areas after the immediate threat to the child has passed. The area of feeding may present as particularly difficult in the recovery period.

Clinical intervention

When a child has feeding difficulties, the mother's inability adequately to feed her child may appear to professionals as the mother's incompetence, or negative attitude or hostility towards her child, or even the withholding of food. If the support offered by professionals is focused solely on changing the mother's behaviour, and the behaviour is not amenable to change, such conclusions may lead professionals towards child protection procedures.

A psychoanalytic approach would concentrate on the clinician forming with the mother a reliable, respectful, therapeutic relationship. Within this relationship, they could work over time on an exploration of the meaning of the current feeding difficulty in the context not only of the infant's young life and possible ill health, but also of the mother's own life experience, including relevant difficult or adverse events. Importantly, the child's nutritional intake and growth and development would be carefully and consistently monitored while the work is being done both with the mother and with mother and child together.

So, a family approach, informed by psychoanalytic understanding of the difficulties, would also explore with the mother her current experiences of being consistently supported and validated in her new and challenging role as parent by a partner or available extended family members.

Clinicians may find that such an exploration uncovers a picture of isolation in the task of parenting alone, feeling helpless, angry, exhausted, misunderstood, and adversely judged by family members, or by a partner who is remote or otherwise excluded from the day-to-day struggles and challenges of parenting.

For example, these negative feelings of uselessness or anger may not be explicitly acknowledged and expressed by the depressed, struggling young mother of a new baby, for fear of being judged or blamed. However, if her feelings are instead communicated to the therapist through projection, or via the transference and countertransference, if not clearly understood, the therapist may act them out in the therapy. So, the therapist may come to experience uncomfortable projected feelings of uselessness and hopelessness in relationship with the mother who is struggling to feed her child. If not understood and managed through clinical support and regular appropriate supervision, the therapist's difficult feelings may be acted out by concluding that there is no point in continuing the therapeutic work. The therapist may angrily decide to end the therapy, and make a child protection referral to social services.

Therapeutic work with the mother and infant would also include other family members if available: for example, the mother's partner or her own mother/parents with whom the therapist would develop a picture of the difficulties experienced by the mother specifically since the baby's birth. The baby's father, particularly, would support the mother's emotional state and offer help through sharing and containing a range of difficult and conflicting feelings. The family might learn for the first time of the mother's isolation, distress, and feelings of incompetence and helplessness, compared to the effective and efficient professionals.

From the extended family, a picture can be compiled of beliefs in the family about food, eating, and feeding babies that might illuminate the mother's current predicament. The family may be able to offer support and respite once they understand the situation more clearly. A dialogue might be facilitated between the new mother and her own mother/parents on family beliefs about parenting.

From conversations between the infant's parents, a picture can be built up of any tensions or difficulties in their relationship that are currently impinging on and inhibiting the mother's relationship with the baby. Perhaps more importantly, the mother can hear clearly from the father what he would be able to contribute, both as support to her and also directly in sharing the care of the baby. Any feelings by the partner of being excluded by the mother, who may thus unintentionally increase her isolation, can also be explored. Outside pressures can be discussed with the couple, such as a financial requirement for the mother to return to work as soon as possible whether or not they want that. This may be contributing to the mother unwittingly creating a distance between herself and the baby in preparation for her return to work, which may be creating problems in the formation of a harmonious feeding relationship.

Such problems, if not recognized, may persist for several years without appropriate professional intervention (Briggs, 2000).

Family one

Margaret, an eight-year-old who does not eat enough

Margaret lives with her mother, father, and new baby brother.

She was referred to a child and family mental health service by a feeding clinic because of failure to progress with weight gain. A referral had already been made to social services because of concern by some professionals that Margaret's lack of progress with her weight was affected by her mother's negative view of her and difficulty supporting her with eating. Margaret's paediatrician felt strongly that she should have a gastrostomy to promote weight gain.

Soon after birth, Margaret had been diagnosed with multiple food allergies, causing absorption problems. She was placed on a strict exclusion diet and as an infant had been fed for eight months by naso-gastric tube. Since this time, Margaret had failed to gain adequate weight.

Margaret's father had not been much involved with professionals or with the feeding clinic. He worked long hours and was sometimes away from home. Margaret's mother was supported by her own parents, who had lived nearby, but, following a move of home to a new area, she became isolated.

Following the move of house and school for Margaret, she was reported by her mother to be struggling more with her eating and remained very reluctant to increase her food intake. School said that Margaret's mother sent little for her lunch, but she had no problem with school food and ate hungrily. At the feeding clinic also, Margaret had been reported to enjoy the children's food provided at lunch-time. At school, Margaret was observed to be a quiet and shy girl.

In the referral to child and family mental health services, the feeding clinic reported that staff there had felt increasingly frustrated with the mother because of her inability to feed Margaret. They had observed mother to appear cold and distant, and rather critical and labelling of her child. Staff had worried about the discrepancy between Margaret's reported eating at home and what they had observed. The mother felt criticized, accused, and not understood, and ceased attendance at the clinic.

A child protection referral was then made by those concerned that Margaret's mother's attitude and behaviour were key contributing factors in her difficulties. They reported that she had "dropped out of treatment".

Clinical intervention

Meetings 1–3: offered to the family and attended by mother alone

> A family therapist at the child and family service offered three appointments to the family. The mother agreed to attend one of these meetings alone for the sole purpose of explaining her withdrawal from the feeding clinic, as she felt that the child protection referral was both unnecessary and grossly unjust. She still wanted help with her daughter's eating and her failure to grow, and did not want her to be tube fed again.
>
> The first meeting was characterized by long silences and the mother repeating that she did not really know why she had come. She explained tersely that she had left the feeding clinic because she felt blamed by the staff. She believed they did not understand what she had been through with Margaret early in her life and now judged her for her distress about her frustrating attempts to encourage Margaret to eat, often unsuccessfully.
>
> Following this, the therapist asked what else she would like to talk about and acknowledged how very difficult and painful events had been for her ever since Margaret's birth. "What is there to talk about?" she replied repeatedly. She had stopped the feeding clinic also because Margaret complained to her bitterly about missing school. "And all they did was criticize me anyway," she added at the end of the first meeting. "I always left feeling like the worst mother in the world and that's no good for her or me."
>
> "That's an uncomfortable place to be, and I wonder how you can move on to feeling a little better than that?" the therapist asked at the end of the session. The mother gave a smile. "How much time do you have?" she queried, wryly. The mother decided to attend the two further meetings offered.

At the beginning of the second meeting, the therapist asked the mother how she wanted to use the time and throughout the meeting the focus was not at all on her daughter's eating difficulties. The mother commented on this difference as previous meetings had concentrated almost exclusively on Margaret's issues and, she felt, on her shortcomings as a mother. "I know this made me defensive and rather argumentative," she concluded.

The mother talked with emotion for almost half an hour about Margaret's early time in hospital, the diagnoses of multiple allergies, her rigid diets, and the horror of holding and restraining her with nurses while she screamed during several frightening and painful diagnostic tests. Her husband had been working away at the time, and so was unable to be with her. The return to a hospital for help with Margaret's eating had been a further trauma for her that brought back a number of unpleasant memories which she had tried to forget.

The mother ended the meeting in tears, saying that she was now back at hospital with her new baby son, who had just been diagnosed with the same problem. She emphasized her weariness and despair and sense of isolation with these stresses and worries. She could not believe that this was happening again. "It's just not fair," she said. "I'm beginning to wonder if it is my fault, like they said."

The session ended with the therapist inviting the mother to tell more of her story at the same time the following week. The mother agreed.

At the beginning of the third meeting, the therapist simply commented on the mother's isolated journey with the difficult, traumatizing events with Margaret, which remained clear in her memory and were now being repeated with her second child. The mother confirmed how lonely she had been; her husband and family had wanted to help, but they did not understand and now she did not want them to be involved. She felt so alone with her children and their difficulties.

She explained that professionals had not understood how traumatized she had been by the early years of caring for Margaret when she would not feed or would be sick, and by the horror of taking part in the awful investigations that her daughter had to endure. She shook as she remembered again how she had held and restrained her while she struggled and screamed. She commented that it seemed like yesterday and she could feel her sweaty head against her and hear her howls. She wondered if Margaret would ever forgive her. "I wonder when you will forgive yourself," the family therapist queried. "How can I when they make me feel so bad?" was the mother's immediate response.

When invited to say more about the professionals' lack of understanding, the mother emphasized how suspicious they had been that she was not prepared to "force" her daughter to eat when she feared she would be sick and "risk her screams again after all that we've been through". She thought the professionals saw her simply as a bad mother. They did not understand, "they're not interested", that in Margaret's early days she had had to prepare herself that she might not survive. "The doctors told me that." Asked if she still worried about her survival, she acknowledged that she did sometimes, though recognized this as irrational, as she knew that now she would be fine.

"And so I just put up my barriers as soon as they started having a go at me," she continued, in response to a question about not being understood, "and then they told me I seemed rather 'cut off' and not involved with my daughter. I was just making things worse for myself, so I got out of there. Then they reported me."

The therapist invited the mother to return with her husband to see if she could now help him to understand. She said she would try, but thought he would not come. The therapist agreed to write to invite him to the next appointment.

Meeting: mother and father

With mother and father together, mother initially insisted that her husband had never been able to be there with her and that he was therefore unable to understand. "Anyway, I think I wanted to protect you," she added, "it was all just so awful." The father emphasized his overwhelming feelings of being marginal and useless and being torn between his work and his family. "I thought you were coping so well," he emphasized. "I knew that it was hard for you, but I was so afraid of making things worse that I stayed away and work was a nightmare at that time . . . I just got my head down and the blinkers on, I suppose. I am sorry, I am so sorry that I did not realize." The mother looked moved. She said simply that he had not understood, and she had never known what he was thinking and feeling about it all.

Therapist (to mother): "What would it mean for you now if you felt that your husband did understand, even a little?"

Mother (tearfully): "I have always felt so alone with Margaret's problems and wanted to prove that I really was a good mother by being able to bear it and manage all by myself."

Therapist: "Prove to whom?"

Mother: "Oh, just to myself, I think—ironic, because now *they* all think I'm such a bad mother, maybe in some ways because I've tried too hard. I don't think I should do that any more, it's too much and it's not helping Margaret. I need to be firmer with her, I can see that now, and I need your help with that I know" (looking towards her husband).

Father: "I didn't know, I just didn't know. I could see that you were managing fine—or so I thought, and so I left you to it, I felt I didn't know what to do. But I'll be around from now on, I've got a little promotion and so I won't be working away any more. I want to spend time with you and the children now."

At the end of the meeting the couple asked to return for a further couple of meetings, without Margaret at first. They wanted to work out how they together as parents were now going to help her to move on with her eating and growing. Mother thought that she might like to bring her own mother also as additional support for one meeting, which was readily agreed by her husband.

"I might try bribing Margaret and offer to take her to see a film if she eats all her supper for a week," the father joked as they were leaving.

Psychoanalytic thinking

The meetings by the therapist, first with mother alone, then with the couple, and later with Margaret also, were informed by psycho-analytic theory.

Importantly, the therapist began slowly, non-intrusively and non-blamingly, to gain the mother's trust. The therapist started with the mother's own experience, and gave her the space and opportunity to air her issues. They discussed the withdrawal from the feeding clinic, but with the therapist having no views about the rights and wrongs of this, but hearing and seeking to understand the mother's experience. The mother repeated her explanations for her behaviour with therapist listening and accepting. The therapist then invited her to relate more of her own traumatic earlier experiences with Margaret, how that felt for her then and now, and how that linked with the current difficulties.

This formation of an open, non-judgemental relationship between therapist and the mother was an essential beginning for the work to proceed in a helpful way.

In the second and third meetings, with the mother alone, the therapist again implicitly and explicitly gave time and value to the mother's own experience, initially at the time of Margaret's birth, early hospitalizations for investigations and diagnoses, and more recently with her continuing difficulties. The mother had never really spoken previously about this in any detail. She was clearly still very affected by what had happened a number of years earlier. She continued to worry about Margaret and to defend against her worries, as she had in the past by distancing herself and keeping her emotions on a tight rein; she thought that this was what a good mother would do and would not make a fuss. When the focus had previously been on Margaret's feeding and mother's difficulties with this, her concerned control and measured coping style had been mistaken for coldness and detachment from her daughter. Gradually, as she began to speak of her worries and traumas, both past and present, she visibly relaxed and warmed in her interactions with Margaret in subsequent family meetings. As she began to speak with her partner about these experiences, she came to feel less alone.

Importantly, the therapist addresses with mother the mother's projection of her negative, self-critical parts into clinicians in the feeding clinic. When mother began to acknowledge and re-own her self-accusations and former ambivalence towards her child, these feelings became available to examination. Mother could then begin to forgive herself for past difficulties and to move on.

The inclusion of maternal grandmother for one meeting with both parents and Margaret proved helpful. It was arranged at mother's request and because it was described that grandma could boost mother's belief in her parenting and in herself. At this meeting, the therapist asked simply how each person, including grandma, thought that he or she could be supportive to the family now, and particularly with Margaret's eating. All had a number of positive suggestions, including Margaret, who thought that granny should come round every week with one of her special chocolate cakes, which she had not had for a while.

Family two

Jamie, a six-year-old who is reluctant to feed orally

Jamie lives with his mother and sister, eighteen years, who remains at home but lives independently.

Jamie was referred to child and family mental health services as he had been fed by gastrostomy since infancy and strongly resisted moving to oral feeding. As a young infant, he had been diagnosed with severe gastric inflammation causing intermittent pain on feeding. He had failed to thrive.

Jamie's parents had separated, with father living and working nearby. He visited occasionally, but did not stay at the family home. His absence from the home was attributed both to mother's depression and to the very close bond between Jamie and mother, which father found difficult and he felt excluded. Mother spoke very little English, even after twenty years in London, but understood some, and an interpreter was required for all meetings. She was culturally and socially isolated, as all her family lived in her birth country in South America.

Jamie's paediatrician strongly recommended that he move to oral eating as appropriate for his age, as his inflammation had improved and he could be supported, if necessary, by medication. However, local medical and nursing services found that Jamie's mother was either unwilling or unable to support and encourage oral feeding by Jamie. Indeed, the mother went into school each day to give Jamie a tube-feed at lunch-time, when the other children were having school dinners. She was afraid that if she did not do this, Jamie would have nothing and be hungry. The school had tried to discourage the mother from this, but had been unable to change her behaviour.

Professional discussion was characterized by frustration and anger with the mother, with feelings that the mother's own mental health difficulties were impinging on the health and development of her son. There was a view that Jamie may not move on in the care of his mother because of mother's own depression and that the real difficulty was mother's inability to reduce tube-feeding and not Jamie's reluctance to eat. A referral to social services was considered and remained on the professional agenda.

Clinical intervention

Meeting: offered to family and attended by mother alone

The therapist arranged to meet the whole family. Mother arrived alone with the usual interpreter, whom the mother described with a smile as almost one of the family. She had not brought any members of her family.

The therapist heard of the mother's fears for her son at birth, from the earliest days when she had tried unsuccessfully to feed him, and of the hospital admissions when she had never left his bedside. She described the tube, the gastrostomy tube, as having saved her son's life and continuing to keep him alive today. "And they expect me to pull it out and risk his life now," she exclaimed through the interpreter.

The therapist asked to whom the mother could turn to share her worries, her desperate fears that her son could still die. The mother shook her head and with gesticulations demonstrated her complete isolation in the world. Her family were far away and unaware of her worries. Her husband now rarely came to the family home. In recent years, her daughter had grown up and was enjoying independence and her own life. The mother worried considerably about her, emphasizing that the streets were unsafe where they lived and she did not like her being out late at night. "But what can I do?" she offered, in heavily accented English, with a wry smile.

She said she had to keep Jamie safe and not let him drift away, as had her older child before she realized the dangers and while she was preoccupied so much with Jamie. "He has these awful stomach problems," she said through the interpreter, "he's always going to need me, I'll always have to be close to him."

"So the tube keeps you together and keeps you both safe—it keeps you from being alone and Jamie safe from the streets?" the therapist asked. Mother smiled and agreed that, without the tube, her son also, even at the age of six, might leave her. Then they would both be alone and unable to manage.

The therapist invited the mother to bring her husband and her daughter to the next meeting with Jamie also and the mother agreed to try.

Meetings: Jamie, his parents and sister

Over the next few meetings, the whole family discussed the tube and its place in family life. Father thought the tube had brought Jamie and his mother so close together that they were almost one. However, he thought it had split them apart as a family, and he felt that he had been pushed out, which he did not want. Over several weeks, gradually with the therapist, the four family members arranged themselves differently in relation to each other. They all expressed their wish to manage without the fifth unwanted member, the gastrostomy tube.

Father and the daughter enrolled mother in English classes at a college nearby. She had considered these before, but had never actually attended, which she promised to do now. The classes extended over lunch-time, and the family agreed that Jamie would take packed lunches to school. Father would be available to support him if he needed him.

The two children asked father to come home for supper in the evenings, and he agreed to do this regularly. The daughter said she would be there, too, at least twice a week and some weekends, when she was not working or at college.

Jamie asked eventually to have school dinners like the other children. He thought he might eat more if he felt like them and not on a table alone. He would ask his best friend to sit with him. Father and sister requested that if Jamie used his tube at all, they would help him with it and he should not ask his mother. Jamie agreed to try this as he wanted to move on.

Psychoanalytic thinking

In Jamie's family, the gastrostomy tube's awkward intrusion into family life may be understood and reframed in psychoanalytic terms as a defence against unmanageable anxiety and depression for Jamie and his mother.

On the one hand, the tube keeps Jamie close, indeed attached, to his mother, who is still depressed and isolated in a new country. The tube and Jamie's continuing proximity and dependence are essential comfort for his mother as she struggles with overwhelming loss and depression. They keep her safe in a hostile world. On the other hand, Jamie has enjoyed the close attention of his mother, which protects him from growing up and facing scary streets, like his sister. Once these purposes for the defence (the tube) have been recognized and verbalized, with the essential support of father and sister, the family begins to move on.

Summary

The essence of this work by psychoanalytically informed therapists that could make a difference may, essentially, be the crucial one of "stance". The therapists avoid becoming drawn into challenging oppositional positions in relation to the mothers, or focusing on areas of perceived failure: that is, the children's eating. The therapists are positioned alongside the mothers, hearing and validating their past experiences, particularly as they affect them in their current parenting. The therapists focus not on the difficulties, but, rather, on seeking to understand the mothers' experiences and building on the mothers' "ego" strengths and competencies. Other important family members are drawn in to support this.

Where young children have feeding difficulties, mothers can feel acutely undermined and hopeless about themselves as effective mothers, particularly if the problems persist. In these situations, and also with other difficulties, fathers are especially important in providing support for the mothers by containing their confusion of difficult emotions and anxieties. Lack of availability by fathers may adversely affect the outcomes for children and for mother–child relationships.

Emanuel writes of the mother's experience of "primary disappointment" when her expectation of a healthy baby is not realized:

> ... I have tried to show ... how the experience of "primary disappointment" in a mother when her innate expectation of a healthy baby is not realized can have a profound impact on the attachment process between mother and baby. The mourning process in that situation is seldom completed and the infant not only suffers from inadequate containment of her projections, but is often the receptacle for mother's projections of disappointment and loss. [Emanuel, 1997, pp. 300–301]

This response applies in both family examples above, as the children have had neonatal hospital admissions for early problems in thriving. Both mothers had anxious, traumatic times with their young infants, unsure what was wrong, fearful that their child may not recover, and feeling isolated. If problems persist into childhood, and if feelings remain split between parents, the mother's fears and worries about being a bad parent may continue. Mothers regularly blame themselves for their infants' problems, and can be overwhelmed by feelings of guilt and hopelessness. Parents need skilled support to hold, contain, and begin to understand a confusing mixture of primitive and conflicting feelings and to share these with each other. They may also need to cope with a sense of loss for the child they did not have, in order to move to a more positive perspective.

Kerbekian writes of work on a premature baby unit, which may apply also to therapy with families in this chapter:

> There are a host of other ways in which the mother and her partner may try to deal with this sudden and overwhelming shock, e.g. by denial or emotional and physical withdrawal. . . . I think it particularly important that they have a person to talk to who is professionally trained to understand and help them cope with these feelings. [Kerbekian, 1995, p. 56]

Through the therapy, both with mothers alone and with couples, the primitive fundamental anxieties in relation to their sick babies can be acknowledged. Links with the parents' mixture of feelings of love, hate, fear, insecurity, dependence, and ambivalence can be recognized and become available to exploration. If the feelings are more available, defences against them become less necessary.

Therapists' knowledge of defences, which seem to protect, and of containment, which holds and keeps safe, allows an understanding of mothers as anxious, fearful, ambivalent, and, sometimes, still traumatized, rather than as cold, distant, and unsatisfactory parents.

CHAPTER FIVE

Children and adolescents with anorexia nervosa

I t is a noticeable feature of current work with children and adolescents with anorexia nervosa that children are now being diagnosed as young as eight or nine years of age. The reasons for this are not clear. The incidence of anorexia nervosa in younger children may be the same as, or similar to, that in the past. Earlier diagnosis could be attributable to an increase in specialist services for children, with anorexia nervosa consequently being recognized in children at a younger age. On the other hand, the numbers of younger children with anorexia nervosa may have increased, possibly because of children's exposure at a younger and younger age to fashion and glamour magazines where their idols are presented both as desirably stick-thin and as role models to be emulated.

In a climate of consumerism, competition, and emphasis on fashionable appearance, young children have become increasingly vulnerable. Recent research does identify the negative influential effect on young girls of under-weight glamorous celebrities, such as fashion models, actresses, and pop singers, and on growing boys of sports and film stars (Hargreaves & Tiggemann, 2002; Tiggemann, 2005). Speaking of a picture of a very skinny model, "Images like this didn't make me an anorexic. But they helped" (Freeman, 2000, p. 1).

The clinical criteria for a diagnosis of anorexia nervosa in *DSM-IV* include weight below 85% of what is expected for age; obsessive interest in food, calories, weight and shape; distorted body image and fear of fatness; restriction of food intake in order to lose weight. That these features may be present in children as young as eight, nine, or ten years of age is, of course, shocking.

No cause for anorexia nervosa has been identified, though some contributory factors may give an indication of aetiology. It is generally accepted that some young people may have a genetic or biological vulnerability to anorexia nervosa. This combines with certain constitutional or personality factors, together with an environmental event, experience, or trauma, to trigger the illness. Other personality, family, social, or environmental factors may play a part in the continuation of the illness (Bryant-Waugh & Lask, 1995).

There are also few categorical answers on the most effective forms of treatment for this group of patients with early onset (under eighteen years) anorexia nervosa.

The current research findings indicate family-based therapy as the treatment of choice for anorexia nervosa of less than two years' duration in children and adolescents (Eisler et al., 1997; Lock, Le Grange, Agras, & Dare, 2001; Russell, Szmukler, Dare, & Eisler, 1987). Treatment trials reported some, though not robust, evidence of conjoint family-based therapy as effective treatment. Alongside this model of family therapy, individual therapy is regularly offered for the young person, in accordance with the UK National Institute of Clinical Excellence (NICE) recommendation that a separate space is available for the young person alone. Research has not yet compared outcomes in the same level of service for family treatment alone with those for family and individual therapies combined. No research has yet included qualified child psychotherapists. An example of the specific integration of individual and family therapies is given in the treatment of Lizzie, below.

Research trials are currently investigating multi-family therapy as intervention and possible alternative treatment to inpatient admission for some young people. These trials have not been completed, and findings are yet to be reported (Asen & Schmidt, 2005). In this model, the therapeutic process takes place with a number of families together, with at least two therapists. There are clear benefits of families helping, supporting, encouraging, and understanding each other. However, there may not be space in this therapy alone for the exploration and development of the more private and individual aspects of family life, or of the internal struggles and conflicts within individual family members.

There are different ways of understanding an eating disorder, and specifically anorexia nervosa, and what it might mean for the young person. It may indicate difficulty in self-regulation of emotions (Schore, 1994) or lack of mentalization (Fonagy, 2004) in response to difficult events. Where there is lack of capacity to mentalize (identify, own, name, and describe feelings), young people may employ defences to try to manage emotional experience for which they are unable to create a coherent account. In this situation, control may be used as a way of bearing the conflict of feelings, and the eating disorder may seem to help the young person to retreat from life events, challenges, and transitions, or consequences of trauma, all of which are experienced as overwhelming and just too difficult. But the young person becomes stuck, and unable to achieve developmental progress.

An eating disorder may be seen from a developmental perspective as a child's way of avoiding a seemingly inexorable progression into adolescence and the advance of sexual maturity. It may be understood as a response to a difficult or problematic relationship with a parent or between parents, where the patient may seem to be rescued by one parent or, indeed, by the illness itself. It may be thought of as a growing child's withdrawal from the developmental task of separation from mother, with particular concerns for the child if there is a troubled parental relationship. It may also be viewed and worked with as a powerful, though inappropriate, communication of distress by the patient to their parent(s) and, indeed, to the outside world.

The growth of feminism from the 1970s highlighted social and power inequalities between men and women, which contribute to women's negative feelings towards themselves, their bodies, and food. "Anorexia and other eating disorders in women are now often attributed to women's obsession with the control, or lack of control, they are able to exercise over their lives" (Sayers, 1986, p. 127). So women, who sacrifice themselves to others, are thought of as keeping under control their own neediness as well as that projected into them by men by controlling their bodies and keeping themselves excessively thin (Sayers, 1991, p. 13).

Over the past couple of decades, professionals working with young people with anorexia nervosa and their families have moved to a different view, both of the illness's origin and of what is helpful to promote recovery. Contemporary family therapy literature highlights the importance of professionals working together as a team in collaboration and co-operation with parents and families, helping patients, together with their families, to work towards their own solutions. Parents are no longer considered to have been implicated in causing their child's illness, as there is, indeed, no evidence to support this view. They are, however, now very much identified and included as an essential part of the solution and treatment team and of returning their child to health (Lock, Le Grange, Agras, & Dare, 2001; Russell, Szmukler, Dare, & Eisler, 1987).

However, despite this collaborative stance of therapists with the families of children with anorexia nervosa, parents continue to present for treatment feeling to blame for their child's illness. An important part of early therapy sessions now is an explicit period of work with parents aimed specifically at relieving them as much as possible of feelings of guilt and blame, which are burdensome and may inhibit the move towards a freer understanding of the illness and towards their child's recovery.

Particularly when a young person has severe anorexia nervosa, parents attend for therapy with stories of their child's repeated rejection of food, often over a long period of time. The more parents try unsuccessfully to feed their child, the more they come to feel useless and rejected and impotent generally in their role as parents. Mothers, particularly, feel an acute sense of hopelessness and rejection, and report feeling upset with themselves for being inadequate and useless. They feel depressed and guilty and despair of their fitness as parents. As parents feel worse, the feeding task appears more challenging and impossible. Working to counter this process and restore in parents a strong sense of their competent and functioning selves is a crucial part of the early family sessions and is central to the whole family treatment process. Parents can be repeatedly prompted to remind themselves of their competences and successes as parents so that they feel strengthened and better placed to support each other and their child against the anorexia nervosa.

Psychoanalytic theory can contribute to thinking about anorexia nervosa from the young patient's point of view. The illness may be understood as a way of managing unbearable feelings and events when attempts to cope via projection into a parent are not effective.

For example, a young adolescent daughter may attempt, through acting-out behaviour,

- to project into her mother feelings of rejection and distress about her unhappy friendships;
- the mother is stressed and preoccupied both by overwork and by the increasing daily needs of a younger disabled child;
- she is unaware of her daughter's friendship difficulties and her particular need for her mother's time and attention;
- she does not understand her daughter's new worrisome behaviour and is unavailable to the projection;
- the daughter is alone with her feelings, by which she is overwhelmed, and feels better when she does not eat.

Alternatively, the illness may be understood as the young person's defence against unmanageable unconscious projections by a parent in response to challenging events in the parent's life. The events may be major losses or traumas, or simply disappointments or unacceptable life events, such as job loss or marital disharmony, for which the adult is ill equipped to cope at that time.

For example, a mother may unknowingly project into her daughter

- her own feelings of distress and overload;
- the mother feels criticized at work and in her marriage;
- she becomes unusually niggly and critical of her daughter, causing the daughter distress which is not recognized and which she cannot manage;
- her eating is affected;
- she feels more in control and further reduces her food intake.

In this way, anorexia nervosa in a young patient can be understood as a physical manifestation of "no-entry" defences constructed to protect from excessive and unmanageable psychic and emotional overload. A sense of being overwhelmed can occur in family situations of multiple life transitions or challenges, or when day-to-day stresses are just too much to bear (Williams, 1997).

An important component in treatment is relationships, and, importantly, the relationships between the young person and parent(s). Psychoanalytic theory understands that these relationships in the present evoke echoes and residues from early formative infant–parent interactions from the past. Perhaps more importantly, psychoanalytic theory offers the idea of a meeting of the internal worlds of the patient and the parents in family relationships in the therapy room.

The therapy might also include bringing aspects of the young person's current troubling inner experience from her individual therapy into family meetings. Through the development of emotional communication, family members can explore with the therapist the correlation between the young person's internal worries and conflicts and her relationships with parents. (See "Lizzie", below.)

Family one

Clara, a fifteen-year-old with anorexia nervosa

Clara lives with her parents and brothers, aged seventeen and thirteen years.

Her treatment for anorexia nervosa comprised individual therapy plus family meetings with a psychiatrist and trainee. She attended family meetings always with both parents and sometimes with her brothers. The trainee was about to leave, and a family therapist was asked to join the family meetings. The psychiatrist felt stuck and was very concerned about Clara's lack of progress.

In team discussions, the therapists had spoken often of Clara's mother's high anxiety. Father was very supportive in helping with her worries. He presented as much calmer, though also concerned about his daughter, who was very ill and struggling to make progress from a low weight.

Between meetings, the clinicians regularly received lengthy phone calls from Clara's mother. She wanted to discuss her worries about Clara's refusal to eat, her moods and aggressive behaviour towards everyone, and their level of stress. Mother found support and reassurance from the phone calls. However, the clinicians were finding her continuing worries and the number of phone calls difficult to manage in busy schedules. They had suggested a number of times that Clara's mother should ask her doctor for medication for her anxiety.

Clinical intervention

The UK NICE guidelines for eating disorders recommend that treatment for children and young people with anorexia nervosa is a family-based intervention specifically addressing the eating disorder.

This guideline was being followed by the clinicians with Clara's family. Each week they focused, as recommended, with the family on Clara's eating, what had been successful and what had been difficult. They addressed the issue of location of responsibility, and identified what might need to change for Clara to make progress. They discussed other issues of concern as they were presented by the family. Each week the family reported that they had worked on the agreed plan: some things improved, but the overall picture remained the same—Clara struggling and fighting with her parents and mother becoming more and more anxious. Mother's anxiety, in turn, had a negative effect on Clara's capacity to make any changes. While mother said she relied heavily on the continuing phone calls, generally she remained fairly quiet in the therapy meetings.

Two meetings: Clara and her parents

The first family meeting with the family therapist was rushed, as the family had been delayed parking and the psychiatrist was held up in another meeting. It took some time to find the room key, then to clear debris and arrange the chairs into the correct circle for the meeting. Clara attended with her parents.

Following an update by father, the family reported on the plan agreed the previous week, which they had followed. However, they had had a terrible week of arguments, with the parents experiencing non-stop opposition from Clara in everything that they tried to support her in achieving.

Towards the end of the meeting, the mother, who had said little, began to cry and to speak of her worries for the future and for the family, who were in distress. She had to be cut short, as the room was booked by another clinician, and the meeting ended rather abruptly.

The family therapist offered to phone next day. On the telephone, the mother talked almost non-stop and did the same when they spoke two days later. The therapist asked each time if she had discussed her worries with her husband, and the mother said that she would do so.

Just before the next meeting, the family therapist spent some time preparing the meeting room, clearing toys and drawings, and setting out the "room within a room" of the correct number of chairs in a circle. She had already phoned her co-therapist to suggest meeting to prepare ten minutes before the appointment. The co-therapist arrived three minutes before the appointed time (as the family were arriving) and the therapists had a couple of minutes together before meeting the family in the waiting room at exactly the right time. There was a noticeably different feeling of relative calm as they walked to the meeting room, which the family found neatly prepared for them. The meeting started on time.

As agreed in the two minutes' preparation time, the therapists started by inviting the family, and specifically mother, who looked bursting to talk, to "Go". The mother spoke for about twenty minutes with barely a pause. Each time she hesitated to collect her thoughts, the therapists asked if her husband shared her worries, and encouraged both to continue, which mainly mother did. After another ten minutes, mother stopped and smiled. "Gosh, that's better, someone else's turn now." Clara and her father laughed and added some comments of their own on the preceding week, which largely agreed with the mother's view. They reassured her that some things were not quite as bad as she had described.

The meeting was almost over when the therapists checked "anything else?" and the family responded that there was not, before finishing.

After the meeting, the psychiatrist commented to the family therapist that he had felt rather useless, as he had been unusually quiet during that meeting. They considered and understood this as his different stance of taking on some of the helpless feelings in relation to the anorexia. This allowed the family, and predominantly mother, to experience some relief. They concluded that this was positive and important progress in treatment, with the family less and less, and the therapists more and more, experiencing the feelings of uselessness. They agreed that in future meetings, the psychiatrist would not act differently simply in order to feel more useful.

They recognized that therapists importantly support families to increase their own sense of agency, competence, and effectiveness, and so render themselves increasingly superfluous. An important part of the work for therapists is identifying and managing their own feelings of increasing redundancy. This was an important point in the therapy. With Clara's mother given space to vent her worries in the therapy room, the phone calls between meetings reduced, and then became unnecessary. The therapists continued to be less active in the room and, with them bearing feelings of relative passivity and "uselessness", the family went on to become more active in the search for their own solutions.

Psychoanalytic thinking

Analytic setting. The time-, place-, and person-specific setting of psychoanalytic sessions can be a key factor also for therapists working clinically with families. (See Chapter Three, "Time and place"). In this example of two family meetings with Clara, the process of the therapy itself was central in effecting change. What the therapists said in the meetings was of relative lesser importance, except for their invitation to mother to talk about what was on her mind (similar to psychoanalytic "free association") and to father to voice his worries also.

Punctuality of time-keeping and preparation of the meeting room tells the family clearly that they have been thought about and kept in mind by the therapists between sessions and prior to this meeting. This, in itself, is holding and calming of high anxiety. Unprepared, rushed therapists may communicate to the family that the therapists are barely managing their own stress and anxiety, and that therefore the family can be thought about only when the session should already have begun. Hence, the worried phone calls between meetings. Clara's mother and her worries were contained by a clear demonstration of being held in mind.

This style of family meeting can provide for a family in crisis an experience of calm acceptance and containment that they have lacked in recent times. This can help and allow them to rediscover some of their natural family equilibrium and usual ways of managing. The regular and accepting style of meeting may also give the family a feeling of being held and their anxieties managed.

Additionally, this containing therapeutic environment allows the family to experience safely a range of feelings: at times, a lack of competence in relation to their sick child, and at other times, feeling useful and effective as they help her to manage and move on. The extremes of emotion are gradually mollified, and in time recede as the family return to previous competent functioning.

In parent–infant relationships, a function of parents is to act as container and processor of projected feelings and experiences that are unmanageable for young children. "Good enough" parents will process these projected feelings and return them to infants in manageable form. Similarly, a function of therapists is to hold the feelings of families, to understand and process them, and facilitate their safe inclusion in therapy for discussion in manageable form.

Family two

Lizzie, a thirteen-year-old with anorexia nervosa

Lizzie lives with her parents, brother aged eight, and sister aged four, with a sister aged nineteen away at university.

She had recently been diagnosed with anorexia nervosa of sudden, severe onset, and was referred to a specialist outpatient eating disorders service for adolescents. She began individual and family therapy when already low weight, sad, distressed, and very angry with her parents for their attempts to feed her. The parents declined to have the younger children involved in any of Lizzie's treatment, though her older sister attended family meetings when at home.

Lizzie was reported by her parents to have been distressed at five years old by the birth of her brother, whom she had described as having taken away her childhood. When this was discussed in the therapy room, Lizzie had become tearful, snapping angrily that she had always loved her brother. The parents thought that she felt that she had to become "grown up" when he was born, as she had felt acutely the loss of her position as the baby and of her special place in her father's affections; she thought that he preferred a male child.

There were serious concerns about Lizzie's declining physical state and failure to progress.

Clinical intervention

Early family meetings in the specialist service were characterized by Lizzie's total lack of any verbal contribution. Her face was shrouded by a curtain of matted hair that fell forwards as she curled up, hugging her knees and shaking. She responded at times with screams, grunts, and sobs as her parents talked of the horrors of the week, their attempts to persuade her to eat, and her angry and sometimes violent refusals. She became upset and scratched at herself in the room when her parents referred to their own arguments. Lizzie was still and quiet only when they talked of the distress of the two younger children.

In parents-only time, Lizzie's parents reported their twenty-one-year marriage as never happy or harmonious. They seemed bemused at having married each other, and described the marriage as a mistake from the start. They thought that their oldest daughter had been relieved to leave home. Recently, their relationship had been more openly conflictual, which they attributed to the stress of Lizzie's ill health. They said that previous therapists had concentrated more on their marriage difficulties than on Lizzie's falling weight, and they had felt very blamed. Father had briefly left home, and returned just after Lizzie became ill because of concerns about her. He had reassured her that he would not leave again.

In her individual meetings with a specialist nurse, Lizzie was also initially silent, though without the behaviours and sounds present in family meetings. The therapist invited her to draw, which she did, and the therapist drew with her. They drew together different feelings such as anger, sadness, and happiness. The therapist encouraged Lizzie with her own examples and quickly Lizzie was regularly drawing emotions, situations at home, and thoughts and feelings about family members. As her therapist put words to her drawings, Lizzie began to speak of her distress about the family, mainly the problems between her parents. She thought the problems would lead to separation, and showed great distress when talking about this. She worried considerably about what would happen if her parents separated, and particularly about her younger siblings, to whom she was devoted and protective. She worried that the three would not stay together, as she thought that "they will tear us apart too". She was afraid that dad would take her brother with him and this possibility distressed her considerably. She knew her brother and sister were worried too. She thought her illness in some ways provided relief from worries about the parents. "Though they [parents] think everything's my fault, they can't see what they are doing to us all."

She was worried and angry with her parents as their arguments continued, but they focused everything on her. "But I know how to make them worried and angry too," she concluded one day with her therapist. "I'll just keep refusing to eat, they can't make me and then they'll know how it feels, won't they?"

Meeting four: Lizzie, her parents and older sister

Lizzie idled into the room behind her mother and grasping at her father's hand. She seemed a much younger child. "Don't bother with him, a waste of time," the mother said to the therapist, indicating her husband over her shoulder.

Lizzie stood at the side of the room until her parents had settled and then immediately jumped on to her father's chair, where she remained squashed beside him. This had become Lizzie's habitual behaviour in family meetings. She said very little during the meeting and snuggled beside her father. At times, father and Lizzie spoke together softly in voices too low for anyone else to hear. Lizzie smiled shyly and whispered into his ear.

The parents barely referred to each other, sometimes contradicting with obvious irritation an opinion of the other. At times, they sighed with clear annoyance towards the other, indicating to the therapist a barely disguised inability to tolerate each other at all.

Mother: "We feel that there is something worrying her but we cannot work out what it is, she won't tell us, we can't think of what it might be, we are all so close and we are all so worried about her."

Family therapist: "Yes, you are clearly a very close family who care so much about each other. Children often have the biggest worries about those to whom they are the closest. For example, when parents argue, children can have all sorts of worries that something awful will happen, perhaps that a parent will leave. Then they may feel very worried and angry."

Father: "We have been arguing a lot recently, but only about Lizzie. She does worry about us arguing, I know."

Older Sister: "She's fed up with the two of you, all you do is squabble."

Lizzie seemed to offer particular comfort to her father at the times when he received contradiction or criticism from her mother. Her sister asked Lizzie to sit by her, but Lizzie declined with a shake of the head.

Alternating with different parts of the story, the parents repeated the history of their daughter's declining health and her current situation.

Father: "We just want our happy chatty little girl back, she used to be so cute."

Family therapist: "Do you want a cute little girl or a teenage Lizzie, who may be loud and argumentative and no longer your happy little girl? Would that be progress but perhaps a challenge for you as parents?"

Mother (with a grin): "I was a nightmare when I was her age."

The parents were able to acknowledge to each other a shared concern about Lizzie.

Psychoanalytic thinking

Lizzie has found her worried and angry feelings about her parents' arguments and threats of separation too much to bear. As the oldest child now at home, and approaching adolescence, she takes on the burden of these concerns. She also worries about her younger siblings and their future together if her parents do separate. She is overwhelmed and her eating is affected. This brings an angry, worried response from her parents, and Lizzie experiences some relief from her emotional overload. So, via her eating difficulties, Lizzie has "projected" her angry, worried feelings into her parents, who have been brought back together and now experience these emotions.

A task for therapy is to help Lizzie to take back, own, and be able to bear her feelings of worry and anger before then being supported in moving on to communicate and discuss these with her parents. The task for the parents is to find a way to work together to help Lizzie, while their own relationship is so conflictual.

Meeting five: Lizzie, her parents and older sister

Father carried in Lizzie, who was whimpering and hiding her face from her mother as she talked to her crossly about a drink she had not finished. "Leave her alone, she's still full after lunch," father told his wife, who looked annoyed as she put the drink away. When the parents had sat down, father offered his lap and Lizzie hesitated before jumping up.

Lizzie's mother began to update the therapist on the previous week. It had been really difficult, with Lizzie regularly refusing to eat and sometimes to drink. She thought that Lizzie would need to be admitted to hospital, though she did not want this as she was young and would need to be in a specialist unit some distance from home. They just could not understand what was bothering her.

Lizzie's father had been quiet, though he whispered occasionally to Lizzie, who seemed almost asleep. The therapist asked if he agreed with his wife, who was invited to repeat to her husband what she had just said. He did not agree, and thought his wife had been hard on Lizzie. He found that a gentler, more encouraging approach was often more effective. "Letting her do what she wants, he means," the mother offered, "he's terrified of making her cross with him, he just wants to spoil her all the time."

Sister: "Why don't you let her sit on her own chair? She's too big for your lap."

Father (barely listening): "She's OK." Sister looks annoyed.

Therapist (to sister): "How can your parents be helped to hear you when you are trying to support your sister in growing up?"

Sister (to father): "Let her sit by me here, what's wrong with you?"

The father hesitated and seemed doubtful. Lizzie opened her eyes and sat up, looking at her mother, who retorted, "He babies her, she's his comfort blanket, he won't let her stand on her own two feet."

Sister: "Don't you start, just let her sit in her own seat," looking at Lizzie and patting the chair beside her.

Father ignored his wife's blatant criticism and nodded towards his older daughter. Lizzie moved without protest from his lap to the empty chair between her sister and her mother. She sat quietly for the remainder of the appointment, occasionally whispering with her sister and her mother.

Lizzie did not interrupt as the therapist discussed with her parents how together, regardless of their difficulties, they were going to ensure that Lizzie took all her drinks and supplements over the next week. Lizzie smiled at her sister at times.

Psychoanalytic thinking

Lizzie's illness has come between her parents, perhaps fortuitously for them as they struggle with their relationship. The strength of her anorexia "splits" them, with each parent accusing the other of being too "soft" or too "hard". The parents are offered a comfortable diversion from the true nature of their quarrelsome disagreements. While the parents are acting out their differences through the illness, the anorexia gains strength.

Lizzie's current behaviour in the room suggests that she is continuing to seek resolution of an early developmental task, which Freud called the Oedipal stage. Lizzie's behaviour indicates a continuing impulse to separate off her father for herself, with the consequent danger of removing her from the possibility of her mother's help and support. It is hardly surprising that Lizzie struggles to relate to her parents as a couple, in view of their acknowledged difficulty in being a couple together.

A therapist who is aware of what Lizzie may be experiencing and the consequent anxiety and stress she is likely to be feeling supports the sister's suggestion that Lizzie takes her own seat. This may serve to relieve Lizzie of her sense of rivalry and power in relation to her mother. She would experience unmanageable anxiety, particularly about growing and growing up, if the generational boundaries continued to be blurred by Lizzie taking mother's place with father. Additionally, by being in opposition to her mother, Lizzie has been deprived of mother's support. Importantly, now she is physically reconnected to her mother in the room and also maintains the support of her sister.

In the context of their hostile relationship, the parents are supported to find a way of relieving Lizzie of her continuing age-inappropriate relationship with father, with whom she had become a powerful "couple" in opposition to mother.

Lizzie is aided by her sister in separating from the fighting parental couple. Her sister's departure from home had left Lizzie alone with her worries and assumed responsibilities for her parents' relationship. With sister as ally, Lizzie experiences some relief.

If necessary, though not in Lizzie's case, siblings can be helped not to become a third demanding parent, as they will sometimes join in the urging of the patient to "just eat". In response to a question by the therapist to the patient whether she would prefer X to be a parent or brother/sister to her, she will invariably say the latter. The family then considers how the sibling can be appropriately helpful.

For example:

Older brother (impatiently to patient): "Why can't you just listen to mum and eat what you are given? I'm just getting so fed up with all this, mum and dad arguing and mum gets so upset."

Therapist (to patient): "Your brother is so good at being another father to you when your dad is unable to attend and even when your dad is here. Is it more helpful to you if he steps in as your father or if he tries to stay your brother with whom you used to have such fun?"

Patient: "I just want him to be my lovely big brother again—it really doesn't help at all when he gets on my case too."

Discussion follows with whole family on activities that patient and big brother used to enjoy together that they can start again. Parents are supported to help brother not to be a parent, not to act or sound like them.

In the case of Lizzie's sister, she is already appropriately linking up with Lizzie both to give her support in staying out of adults' arguments and difficulties and also by example on how to challenge parents in an appropriate way.

Clinical intervention

Lizzie's family and individual therapists had regular discussions between all therapy sessions. They concluded it was important to incorporate into family meetings some of Lizzie's worries about her parents, though she was adamant that she could not discuss the worries with them. She thought they would deny any problem. It was not appropriate for the family therapist to raise these issues, as Lizzie did not give her permission.

The individual therapist discussed with Lizzie over a couple of meetings, with the use of drawings, the possibility of the therapist coming to family meetings with her to help her to share her worries with her parents. After a while, Lizzie agreed to this, with some hesitation and also with a little apparent relief.

While these negotiations were taking place in individual therapy, the family therapist was preparing and supporting the parents in parents-only time for the introduction of Lizzie's worries into family meetings. The therapist worked with the couple as a parenting unit and did not become involved in their relationship difficulties, since this was not requested.

Meeting six: Lizzie and her parents with family and individual therapists

The family therapist opened the meeting by explaining that Lizzie's individual therapist had joined them in order to bring to family meeting some of what they had been talking about in their one-to-one meetings. She confirmed that Lizzie, with her therapist, had agreed what would be shared in the family meeting.

Mother: "We're all for openness, we wondered what they were talking about."

Individual therapist: "Do you want to start, Lizzie, or shall I?"

Lizzie (with head down and face hidden): "You start, I can't say."

Individual therapist: "I'll start and you chip in if I forget or get anything wrong?" Lizzie nods.

Individual therapist: "Lizzie and I have been talking a lot about Lizzie's worries, big worries that she has been afraid to bring up at home."

Father: "We like to be very open, I wonder why she is afraid."

Family therapist: "Yes, we have been talking about openness, which can sometimes be most difficult with those to whom you are closest—perhaps for fear of upsetting them."

Individual therapist: "Lizzie's big worry is that her parents are fighting a lot, all the time, and she has a very big worry that they will separate."

Mother: "We don't 'fight', just arguments really, but you needn't worry, Lizzie, dad won't ever leave again, you don't need to worry about that."

Individual therapist: "Lizzie's big worry was also that you would tell her that there was no need to worry, because she doesn't believe this. She does worry a lot and wonders what will happen to the three of them if you separate, she worries they will be split apart."

Mother and father both look shocked and father a little cross.

Father: "Is this really necessary, is it, you're just worrying her more?"

The family therapist confirmed that the conversation was really important for the family, that Lizzie was worried and did not want to hear that everything was all right because that was not how it felt to her. She emphasized that Lizzie wanted to know from her parents what they planned would happen for the children if they decided not to stay together. She assured the parents that this could be discussed further in family meetings if helpful to them.

Mother: "Yes, I can see that, I can see that that worries her." Looking at father, "Do you want to tell her or shall I?"

Father indicates for mother to continue.

Mother (to Lizzie): "We didn't want to worry you and so we didn't tell you. When dad left last time, he and I made an agreement—in brief, the four of you would stay at home with me and you would see your dad regularly, he would live nearby. We thought that might be better than all the arguments, but we didn't want you to worry. Now we've decided to stay together to get you well."

Lizzie (looking up for the first time): "And so what happens if I do get well, will you split up then?"

Both parents look towards the family therapist.

Family therapist: "Perhaps this is something you would like to discuss in family meetings—how Lizzie can be well without worrying that you will then separate?"

Father: "Yes, more family meetings."

Family therapist: "As Lizzie gets well and grows up, relationships at home may seem in some ways to become more difficult before they get better. She will get lots of help in being a teenager from her big sister. You now know that Lizzie is very aware of your difficulties and she will challenge you to show her how you can stick together as parents to help her to fight this anorexia. She will be watching you to see how you do this so that she can stay at home. What will you show her?"

Psychoanalytic thinking

In all these excerpts, Lizzie and her family have given examples of the defences of projection, denial and splitting.

Lizzie's worries have reached this extent because her parents "deny" to her that there are any problems between them. They do not face their own difficulties and so cause unmanageable anxiety in their daughter. The therapist later learns that both parents experienced in childhood their own parents' separation, and so cannot face this possibility for themselves and their children. Lizzie's illness temporarily rescues them and allows them to put off taking any decision again.

With both therapists supporting the family, Lizzie begins a conversation with her parents on her concerns about them. These worries that have been lodged in Lizzie's head are brought into the whole family. Together with the therapists, and through the development of open dialogue and emotional communication, Lizzie can let her parents know directly of her feelings and concerns and no longer needs to use her worrying behaviour. Having told her parents of these worries, Lizzie is relieved of the burden of maintaining her secret concerns and can work increasingly with her parents to get well.

Part of Lizzie's worry also was that her wish for an exclusive relationship with her father would be too powerful and destroy her parents' marriage. So, the parents meet together in adults-only time with the therapist to work on their togetherness as parents in order to relieve Lizzie of anxiety about her capacity for destructiveness. The parents work also with the therapist on providing good enough parenting together, whether or not they remain a couple. The family will be supported in communicating openly, and not denying the difficulties. The parents will be offered time to work on ways of talking with Lizzie and reducing her worry about the consequences if they do separate. This is consistent with the *sine qua non* of therapy with families of a child with anorexia nervosa—that parents work together to support their child against the illness.

CHAPTER SIX

Children who have experienced emotional harm

E motional harm caused to children by emotional abuse or
neglect by a parent or main carer has been recognized more
widely in the literature in the last couple of decades (Glaser,
2002; Iwaniec, 1995). Emotional abuse may, in some ways, appear
to be a softer and less damaging form of abuse than the more
widely recognized physical and sexual abuse and physical neglect.
While emotional abuse and neglect may cause no physical evidence
or scars, professionals are increasingly aware of their extremely
harmful effects on children's healthy emotional and psychological
development and functioning, their general well-being and happiness, and their social adjustment into adolescence and adult life.

Glaser (2002) categorized emotional abuse and neglect of children in five broad conceptual areas: emotional unavailability; negative attributions; inappropriate developmental expectations; failure
to recognize the child's separateness, individuality, and uniqueness;
mis-socialization.

The number of children on Child Protection Registers (now
Protection Plans) in England rose to 27,900 at 31st March 2007. Of
these, 23% of registrations were for emotional abuse, a rise from
18% in 2002–2003 (Community Care online, 21st September 2007).

For some children, emotional abuse is the sole form of abuse they experience, while for others it is an intrinsic and inevitable component part of other more visible and identifiable forms of abuse— physical or sexual abuse or neglect.

In a number of ways, emotional abuse is different from other categories of child abuse. Specifically, emotional abuse and neglect are established and integral components of the child's relationship with his or her parent. They can be difficult to detect and identify, and the harm to the child has usually persisted over some time and may have caused significant damage before it is recognized.

When emotional abuse is identified, referral can be made to social services, though there may be no clearly defined events or incidents that are available to investigative scrutiny and the situation may not be amenable to the usual statutory child protection procedures, even if appropriate. Any resulting protection plan will require that parents change their behaviour within specific parameters and timescales. Failure to manage change may lead to legal proceedings because of continuing unacceptable significant harm to the child.

Emotional harm to children may have a number of causes: for example, the mental ill health of a parent who is unavailable to meet the child's needs; a parent who drinks too much or takes drugs and is out of control or frightening, and who is unable to meet the child's needs; a parent who does not like a child and who constantly criticizes or humiliates; a parent who is violent to another parent so that a child is fearful for the safety, or even the life, of a loved parent; a parent who expects more or less of a child than the child is able to do; a parent who received poor parenting and tries to repair the past through a child and does not recognize the child's separate and unique identity and needs; a parent who encourages in a child disrespect for authority figures (e.g., teachers or the law).

Significant emotional harm to a child, caused within his or her primary relationship, is assessed as abuse if it is persistent, pervasive, and avoidable, is attributable to the behaviour of the parent, and has caused impairment to the child's functioning or development. This would necessitate change by the parent in the child's best interest. Legal action may be considered if the parent does not acknowledge the harm and is unwilling or unable to change. This is different and more serious than emotional distress or harm caused to a child by an expectable life event, such as parental separation or bereavement, which the parent has been unable to ameliorate, or by a *difficult* but not abusive parent–child relationship. In the latter, a parent's behaviour may be lacking and regrettable, but assessed as "good enough".

Emotional abuse or neglect of a child by a parent may also be understood in psychoanalytic terms as parents working out, through the relationship with the child, their own early unresolved issues. The difficulties may relate to parents' childhood experience with their own parents, or to the birth of younger siblings: relationships that resonate with, and are rekindled by, conflict of feelings in the present. These issues have remained painful, unrecognized, and unresolved. The birth of a child has acted as a trigger for the parent's unresolved past experiences, sometimes leading to the development of an emotionally abusive relationship. This does not condone the difficulties in the parent–child relationship, but it may shed light and make them more available to therapy.

For example, a father may experience, through the birth of his child, the recreation of unresolved feelings of envy and rivalry previously felt in his own childhood at the birth of his younger sibling. His internalized pattern of family relationships in the past (love for a younger newborn girl mixed with envy and rivalry at the monopoly of mother) become mobilized by their resonance with his present conflict of love for his daughter as well as envy and rivalry at her apparent monopoly of mother. He directs towards his child the negative thoughts and feelings and aggressive impulses held previously towards the loved but also envied and believed-to-be-preferred younger sibling. These feelings had not been previously expressed or even consciously recognized.

Or, a mother who felt unwanted or was rejected as a baby may experience unmanageable and unexpressed ambivalence about the conception and birth of her own daughter. She shows this unconsciously by intermittent but continuing emotional unavailability or neglect in relation to her child.

Or, a mother who had considered plans to "get rid of" her baby by termination or adoption, but who changed her mind on the birth of the baby, may continue throughout the baby's childhood to feel over-protective and over-consult medical professionals as a defence against her earlier dismissed but unresolved and frightening feelings of wanting to be rid of her child.

In the examples above, change is required in a parent in order that the harm to the child is discontinued. Therapy to this end may include work with the troubling internal worlds of parents in order to effect change in the adults' behaviour and, thus, in the parent–child relationship.

Family One

Thomas, a twelve-year-old who has been bullied at school

Thomas lives with his mother.

He was referred for therapy following serious bullying at school three months earlier, when he suffered physical injury. Since that time, his mother has refused to send him back to school and she reports that he is frightened to leave home.

The referral to child and family mental health services described Thomas's mother, twenty-eight, as having always been extremely anxious about Thomas's health. As a baby, he had numerous GP and hospital visits and, on one occasion, Thomas was referred to social services because of multiple hospital attendances during a couple of weeks one winter. The social services department visited, but took no further action except to recommend increased monitoring by Thomas's health visitor, which was done for a few months with no further concerns.

Mother's worries about Thomas's health continued, and he missed significant amounts of primary school. His teachers observed him to be an anxious child who worried considerably about minor falls and upsets in the playground. Despite looking fairly robust, he had described himself to his teachers as "sickly" and having "health problems". His behaviour and academic progress were impeccable, despite his frequent absences from school.

Since Thomas's move to secondary school, teachers had raised some worries that Thomas's mother's continuing excessive concerns about his health were making him a target for jokes and teasing at school. His mother was observed to treat him as a younger and very vulnerable boy, to "baby" him, and not to meet and respect his emotional needs age-appropriately.

One particularly cold day in winter, Thomas arrived at school well wrapped up and also cuddling a hot-water bottle, which he refused to give up, saying that he was cold. He reported that his mother had expressly instructed him to keep the bottle with him all day and to request that it was refilled with hot water as soon as it cooled down. She did not want him to catch a chill. During the lunch break, Thomas had his bottle taken from him and emptied over his head by a group of older boys, who ridiculed him. When he became angry and struggled to regain the bottle, saying that he would tell his mum, he was hit and kicked, causing bruises and lacerations which required stitches at hospital.

Thomas's mother had collected him from school to take him to hospital, and he had not returned to school since. Mother said that Thomas would never attend the school again, and she would give up her job in order to home-educate him.

The referral was described as a "last hope" by professionals before involvement again of statutory agencies.

Clinical intervention

Meeting one: Thomas and his mother

At the first appointment with Thomas and his mother, the therapist invited them to offer their understanding for the meeting and who was worried about what.

They sat close together, and mother regularly reached for Thomas's hand, which he did not resist. He kept his head down.

Mother explained that she was very worried about Thomas because he was "delicate" and the school did not seem to understand that. He had been horribly bullied and he was not going back to that school, and now "they have sent us to see you". Thomas said little, but nodded occasionally as his mother spoke. "I think mum's right, I need to go to school but not there, it's too tough for me."

The therapist asked Thomas about being "delicate", what this meant for him.

"Mum worries about me," he replied. "She's so worried about me getting sick; she's a very good mother to me."

Mother smiled and reached for Thomas's hand, which this time he kept in his lap.

The therapist acknowledged mother's and Thomas's helpful account of their troubles. She arranged to meet with mother alone on two occasions, and then to meet with them together again.

Meeting two: Mother alone

At the first meeting with Thomas's mother alone, she was invited to describe her experience of pregnancy and the time around Thomas' birth and his early years.

She then talked almost without hesitation for the following forty minutes, and paused only when reminded that just a few minutes of the session remained. She commented a number of times as she told her story that she had never told anyone this before, had never had the opportunity to describe what had happened and how this time had been for her, when she herself was only in her mid-teens and a schoolgirl. When asked why she thought she had not spoken of this before, she replied simply that no one had ever asked.

Thomas's mother had become pregnant when she was sixteen years old. She was still at school and predicted to do well and go to university, which her parents supported. She told a rather unclear story about falling for an older man she trusted who was said to have "taken advantage" of her. As soon as she was pregnant, he disappeared back to his family. For several months she had considered termination of her pregnancy, until that was no longer an option. She then planned to have Thomas adopted and return to school to continue her hopes for university. However, when Thomas was born, she described with clear pleasure having "despite myself, fallen for him at first cuddle".

Her parents and wider family had put enormous pressure on her to continue the plan for adoption and were very angry with the baby's father. She was angry with them for their attacks on him. Alone, the mother resisted calls to give up the baby. After Thomas's birth, they moved to a mother and baby home for teenage girls, where they lived for two years, and then moved into their own accommodation, where they had remained since. The mother returned to education and had almost completed an Open University degree. She supported herself and Thomas with steady work and promotions.

For the past twelve years she had remained completely isolated from her family, whom she did not see, as she remained angry that they had criticized Thomas's father. "So it's just me and him now, so I've got to look after him." Her parents had contacted her several years previously, wanting to see her and the baby. She had been suspicious and remained fearful that they might still wish Thomas "harm". She harboured continuing thoughts that Thomas's father might still return to her and defended his behaviour against any criticism.

"It was such a shock to be pregnant," she commented at the end of the meeting. "When he left me, I used to wish the pregnancy away, I went to sleep at night and just hoped it would be gone in the morning—but I could not do anything to get rid of him, I could not do that, I think I would never have forgiven myself."

She was invited to come back a week later to continue to tell this story, which she agreed that she would like to do.

Psychoanalytic thinking

Psychoanalytic theory can contribute an understanding of Thomas's mother's excessively over-protective behaviour as her "projection" into the outside world of her own hostile, aggressive impulses, which had remained unrecognized and unprocessed over the previous twelve years or more. She directs these towards her family, whom she sees as hostile and a continuing threat to Thomas, and this has kept her isolated from them. Hence, she remains totally alone with Thomas and her overwhelming worries about his health and well-being. The environment is seen as a constant and enduring source of danger and harm to Thomas; winter is so threatening that Thomas alone requires a hot-water bottle to protect him and ensure his health and survival; school is so threatening that Thomas has to stay at home for the slightest reason of ill health, or even for no real reason at all.

Mother is thus cleared of any negative or attacking feelings and presents as a devoted and totally caring, indeed over-caring, parent who is single-mindedly committed to her child.

Thus the mother who is constantly apprehensive that her baby may die [*or come to any harm*] is unaware of the impulse in herself to kill it [*or get rid of it*] and, adopting the same solution she adopted in childhood perhaps in regard to her death-wishes against her own mother, struggles endlessly and fruitlessly to stave off dangers

from elsewhere—accidents, illnesses, the carelessness of neigh-
bours. [Bowlby, 1989, p. 18, my interpolations in italics]

So, when the school does present a very real and frightening threat
in the form of bullying fellow pupils, Thomas is immediately withdrawn to the safety and protection of the family home, where his
mother plans to keep him and educate him there herself. Mother
holds and displays only caring and loving feelings, but Thomas's
healthy development is being seriously impaired.

Meeting three: Mother alone

When Thomas's mother returned one week later, she was invited to
continue telling her story, which she did.

"I can see now that I have always worried about him so much," she
began, as soon as she had sat down. "Not surprising really, when so
many people, including me at first, were wishing him such awful
harm."

Asked if she could explain what she meant, she thought briefly and
then went on, "Well, there's me and my family planning to end his life
before he is even born and then me and them scheming to get rid of
him as soon as he is born. After I had decided to keep him, and no one
would ever have changed my mind then, I was always terrified that
they would somehow get to him and get rid of him. Perhaps I am still
scared, which is why I wrap him up in cotton wool like I do. It's not
good for a boy I know, but I am so worried for him even now, frightened and angry that harm might be done to him. He is so precious to
me, he's all I've got, I don't know what I'd do if anything happened
to him."

"Have you wondered about the harm done to you?" the therapist
asked. "When have you felt frightened or angry about that?" Mother
startled, asking what was meant. "The harm done to you at sixteen by
the man you trusted who left you. I think you have told me that you
have had good reason to be angry with him." The mother shook and
revealed that she had been terrified when he left and had felt murder-
ously angry with him. She had cried herself to sleep, thinking he would
return. "I know he won't, but I keep on hoping."

The mother went on to reflect further on her continuing futile hopes
that the man would return and became determined that she was ready

to let them go. "And then I took it out on my family," she went on. "I gave my poor parents one hell of a time. I could be angry with them because I knew they would always be there, they would never leave me, but I couldn't be angry with him because I wanted him back." "Wanted or want?" the therapist queried towards the end of the second meeting with mother. "I have to face facts," the mother replied. "I have to move on. I felt so angry with him the other night, I could have smashed his face in. I've enrolled at a gym so I can take it out there! Next time my mum phones, I'm inviting them round."

At the end of the meeting, mother commented that Thomas had never asked about his dad. "Perhaps he just knew that I couldn't speak about him. I think I could now and I'd tell him what I know, if he wants to hear."

Continuing meetings: Thomas and his mother

The meetings with Thomas and his mother dovetailed with those for mother alone in order not to delay work on some pressing family issues. In an early family meeting, mother told Thomas that he should return to school to get his education. He looked surprised, and she reassured him that the bullying had been dealt with. She invited a friend of his to visit, who also encouraged Thomas to return. His friend told him that the bullies had been "sorted out" by the head and he need not worry about going back. His friend emphasized that Thomas must not let his mum make him do "weird" things, like the hot water bottle—"That's asking for trouble, you know."

Thomas accepted his mother's view, saying that he knew he could not hide away from the bullies and had to face them. His friends would help him with any problems. He was adamant that she must stop mollycoddling him too, no more hot-water bottles. His mother agreed and was pleased with his response.

Mother supported Thomas' wish to join the school karate club, which she had previously opposed as being too rough for him. He thought it would give him more confidence and deter any bullies. His friend Charlie had begun karate, and encouraged Thomas to join. Charlie told him the boys talked about Thomas's "odd" mother and how she treated him like a baby. "I am twelve now," Thomas insisted at the end of one meeting. "I want you to stop treating me like that." Again mother agreed, and told Thomas that they were going to move on in their lives as he was growing up now. She was planning to get back to studying and finish her degree and she would go to the gym each week to keep fit.

Psychoanalytic thinking

Further meetings with mother and joint meetings with Thomas continued to focus on mother promoting Thomas's growing up and gradual independence. Thomas was reassured that his mother would be all right and would not be totally isolated without him, especially as she had begun to see her family again.

The therapist's stance in the therapy is again alongside the family and not directly challenging of the mother. The therapist facilitates the mother in reflecting on the origins of her current anxieties about Thomas, both from earlier relationships and previous ambivalence. The therapist demonstrates interest in seeking to unpick and understand with the mother the resonances from the past in the family's current difficulties. Within this safe and respectful relationship, the mother comes to recognize the inappropriateness of her current behaviour and the harm caused to Thomas by her acting out her worries now. She is supported to see the reality and manageability of risk in the outside world, to which she has attributed her internal hostile and aggressive feelings. By being able to acknowledge her early "hostility" towards Thomas and projection of her own angry feelings about his father, again the mother can be supported in taking back and owning the aggression that had been projected into her family and the outside world, leaving the family and world as less scary and attacking places.

The psychoanalytic concept of "displacement" may be helpful. It becomes clear through mother's story that she has suppressed her hostile aggressive feelings towards Thomas's father by "displacing" them on to her own family: they are safer directed there, as she says, as her family can be relied upon and her former partner cannot. The therapist works with her to redirect the displaced feelings, so that mother begins to feel anger and indignation towards the man who has let her down and her family can then become a source of strength and support.

A therapeutic relationship of respect, trust, and acceptance has been developed, within which these painful issues can continue to be safely explored.

Family two

Maria, a nine-year-old whose father is always
criticizing her and putting her down

Maria lives with her parents and her brother, Jack, aged twelve years.

Maria was referred to her child and family service with concerns by school that, though a bright child, she was struggling to keep up with less able children. Early in her school career she had consistently gained high marks, and seemed to enjoy all aspects of school life and was always well motivated. However, over the past couple of years she presented frequently in low mood and tearful for no apparent reason, and sometimes came to class saying that she could not do her homework. She told her teacher recently that her father called her "stupid".

Maria's mother had minimized this, saying that father did not want to put pressure on his children, especially Maria, whom he thought anyway would just marry and have children. Mother acknowledged that Maria seemed very low and unhappy, and agreed to the referral for "counselling" for her.

Clinical intervention

Meeting one: offered to family and attended by Maria and her mother

Maria attended with her mother, without father or brother. Mother explained that Jack had been forbidden to miss school by his father for what he called "a silly waste of time".

The therapist invited Maria and her mother to tell her about their family.

Mother described them as a professional family. Both parents were in their mid-thirties. She had been to university and obtained a good degree in languages, which, with a smile, she said her husband described as "a bit of a soft option". Her husband had not been to university, but began work in a law firm on leaving school and had worked his way up to a good position as a lawyer, studying part-time for a law degree on the way. Maria was born while he was studying hard for his final exams, and he had been stressed and torn between what he had called "conflicting demands on my time and emotions".

"He was not encouraged at all by his parents," mother explained. "He had this very beautiful younger sister on whom his parents doted and they did everything to put her through drama school, which was her ambition. Then she gave it all up when she married and had children. I don't think my husband has ever forgiven her, or them," she added quietly.

Maria listened while her mother talked, and then asked if daddy was cross with her because of Auntie Bev. "He is always so cross with me," she complained tearfully. "He's all for Jack all the time, Jack can do no wrong—and I can get nothing right, it's not fair, it's just not fair."

The therapist thought with mother how her husband could manage to attend a session to discuss the difficulties for Maria. Mother had not tried to persuade him or Jack to attend but preferred to come alone "as Maria gets so upset when her father 'has a go' at her, and I didn't want it to happen again here with you."

"I would like daddy to come," Maria interrupted. "Mummy can tell him how sad I am, that I want to be friends with him, not like this, him being cross with me."

It was agreed that mother would ask father to attend with her next time without Maria, which mother thought would be possible and less distressing for them all. Maria was pleased, preferring to go to school for a special project that day.

Psychoanalytic thinking

> The father who resents the baby's monopoly of his wife and insists that her attentions are bad for it is unaware that he is motivated by the same kind of jealousy that he experienced in childhood when a younger sibling was born. [Bowlby, 1989, p. 18]

The psychoanalytic perspective on father's negativity towards Maria may be helpful. It can steer the therapist away from feelings of anger and wishing to challenge. It may provide an alternative to child protection thinking in a situation where Maria is indeed suffering "significant harm" from the repeated criticism directed at her by her father. A psychoanalytic view might lead towards an understanding of the source of this negativity and, while neither accepting nor condoning it, may provide a way forward by working with the whole family. This needs to be preceded by some work with the parents alone.

Meetings two and three: mother and father

The first meeting began with Maria's father complaining about wasting time at the appointment, with important work missed and Maria being "manipulative" and "simply attention-seeking". He told his wife aggressively that she indulged Maria, giving in to her "whining ways" and what she needed was "a jolly good talking to and just be told No occasionally." He justified his long working hours and late returns home as avoiding "what is going on with you and her".

The therapist asked if mother knew what he meant, and she said that she did not, though perhaps he was referring to her closeness to Maria. The mother listened as her husband continued for a while, with apparent increasing discomfort.

The second meeting began with father's complaints again about the meeting, "a useless waste of time". Mother listened with annoyance, but unable to interrupt.

After a while, the therapist observed to father that he seemed to feel she was not hearing or appreciating his point of view. Maybe she was not providing something for which he was hoping from a therapist and so was wasting his time. She wondered if father experienced her as "taking sides". Perhaps this was not a new feeling for him.

Father continued in argumentative vein, with his wife becoming increasingly outraged until she exploded. He later said that he had never experienced this before and was clearly both affected and significantly shaken.

Maria's mother challenged father with her understanding of the reason for his severity and negativity towards Maria. "She's right," indicating the therapist, "you felt unappreciated at home and thought your parents were always for your sister, you thought they were always on Beverley's side. You've had 'a chip' about that all your life. And then with Maria, you couldn't stand her from birth. Well, you did love her, I know, but you couldn't bear me to pay her attention, or even to care for her, it goaded you because of Beverley." She paused and the therapist asked father this time if he knew what his wife meant. He looked a little bemused, but nodded slowly. Mother continued, more gently as she saw his discomfort, "Your mother neglected you when Beverley was born, your father was never there. They loved you, but they ignored you as soon as she came along and she was the apple of your mother's eye, what your mother herself had wanted to be. It was as simple as that, you were sent off to school to make way for her. You adore Beverley now, but you are taking it out on Maria, who does not deserve the way you treat her, you are taking out your hurt and fury on your own daughter. She is miserable, she adores you and wants you to be with her as you are with Jack. What happened to you cannot be undone, maybe it was no one's fault, your parents believed that they meant well but were misguided in how they behaved towards you."

Maria's father was moved and close to tears, and then angry. The therapist acknowledged the painfulness of the conversation for both parents and also its importance. Father retorted that he had felt pressured by mother to have another child just when he was doing his vital law exams. "You had to be just like your big sister, didn't you?" he questioned her. "There had to be a three-year age gap, just like her, you're so in awe of her, why couldn't we do things our way?" Mother was surprised and stunned, but acknowledged what father had said. She said she had always felt distressed and angry that her sister was the favourite, had never dared say this before and just kept trying to be like her.

The therapist enquired how the couple could support each other with this. They said the conversation had brought a few things home to them, which they would continue to discuss at home. They needed to understand better what was going on in the family, as they were aware that the unhappiness was not just Maria's.

Psychoanalytic thinking

Seeing or understanding an aspect of our own behaviour in itself may not bring about change in that behaviour. Indeed, counter-productively, defences and anxious denials may be aroused until worried feelings and splits are contained. Psychoanalytic insight is different from rational understanding of what might previously have been neither recognized nor understood. Psychoanalytic insight refers to the process of raising to conscious awareness the way in which past experiences or relationships with difficult feelings, which were not resolved or integrated into the developing personality, are being re-created and acted out repeatedly in the present through current relationships in a harmful, dysfunctional way (Yelloly, 1980).

Psychoanalytic insight may be gained in clinical psychoanalytic psychotherapy through, for example, the transference and interpretation. In therapy with families, where the therapist recognizes and values the benefits of insight, the therapist seeks to create the necessary safe and predictable therapeutic space for the exploration of difficulties that may be intruding with negative effect into present family relationships.

In this family example, the therapist clearly recognizes her countertransference feelings of being unhelpful and unappreciating. The therapist does not interpret her countertransference, but simply wonders whether father has experienced previously this feeling of someone not being able helpfully to hear and appreciate him. This is difficult for father to acknowledge, but mother relates the situation back to his adverse family experience as a child.

So, it can then be recognized by the therapist with Maria's family that father had brought into the current relationship with his daughter aspects of his relationship with his sister in the past and the associated feelings that remained with him. Maria's mother had sought to compensate for this by the development of a close and protective relationship with her daughter, from which father felt excluded. Mother had brought sibling rivalry with her older sister into her present family, causing unacknowledged stress and adverse reaction from her husband. The therapist works to help the parents distinguish feelings in old relationships from relationships now in their present family, and to keep feelings appropriately in their place. Maria's father is supported by the therapist in developing a view of his daughter separate from his problematic perspective on his sister many years ago, so that he and Maria can enjoy a different and more positive relationship now. Mother comes to acknowledge with father that she had put her sisterly rivalry ahead of consideration for her husband, resulting in a need for them to address the consequences now.

Father's attendance was clearly important in presenting a different and more rounded perspective on his behaviour towards Maria. The therapist hears from him that mother's pressure, for her own personal reasons, propelled them from a manageable three-person family to an unmanageable, for him, four-person family at a time of particular stress for him. His exams had significant meaning for him in proving his ability to achieve, both to himself and to his parents, and took him away from family life at a time when his wife went ahead with her wish to have a second child. His behaviour towards Maria, which suggests dislike and aggression for her, came from his feelings of pressure and threat from the unwanted dependence and demands on him of another child. Apparent hatred or dislike is frequently connected to feelings of persecution caused by expectations to be someone one cannot yet be, and consequent feelings of failure.

The therapy sessions for parents together facilitate discussion on the contribution of both parents to the difficulties for them at the time of Maria's birth. The mother is supported in acknowledging her part so that the parents can attempt to move on together.

Meetings: Maria, her parents, and brother Jack

The continuing family meetings addressed the task of the family mending the previous mother–Maria/father–Jack split. Jack expressed a wish that his sister join him and his dad in some of their activities when mother was working or otherwise occupied. Father began to help Maria with her homework, whether or not she needed help. They began to prioritize whole-family outings.

Mother and father continued to attend some sessions without the children.

Summary

The important task for therapists of engaging with families, and specifically with parents, may be particularly difficult where children are referred with concerns about emotional harm. There does not have to be intent by parent for their behaviour to be assessed as abusive, or for its effects to be harmful for a child. The abuse may include acts of omission as well as of commission.

The therapist may feel uncomfortable and angry if a parent seems to be abusive, or the therapist may be aware of identifying with the abused child with a wish to rescue and protect. The therapist may wish to discontinue therapy and to refer to social services for investigation.

Good enough safety and protection of the child must be ensured at all times. The therapist with the family may be working alongside statutory agencies carrying out an assessment or investigation. The therapist is challenged to conduct "business as usual" in the development of even-handed relationships with all family members and with the family as a whole. The therapist is clear with the family that any information or behaviour of concern will be reported.

The therapy can then be conducted in the usual style of attentive listening to all, exploring difficulties with the family, non-judgemental response, with a search always to understand and develop a family-specific meaning for the referred behaviour, relationship, or "problem", in order to move towards change.

Professionals may be encouraged by remembering that the majority of parents want help to stop abusing their child. Indeed, they may not have been aware that their behaviour was abusive and harmful (Kempe & Kempe, 1978).

> Perhaps the most interesting findings are that even amongst those who have been abused and neglected in childhood, a proportion are able to provide a coherent narrative of their pain and trauma, and are therefore more likely to benefit from therapy. [Kraemer, 1997, p. 55]

CHAPTER SEVEN

Young children whose behaviour can be violent

The umbrella of emotional harm includes the damaging emotional impact on children of their own violent behaviour, which their parents cannot safely manage and help them to control. Writing of control issues, Fahlberg says,

> If a parent doesn't know how to take charge when a child is out of control, the young person senses this and becomes frightened. He or she keeps setting up opportunities for the parent to learn to take charge. If the parent continues to be unable or unwilling to control the child in such a situation, the child's inappropriate behaviours usually escalate. [Fahlberg, 1994, pp. 297–298]

The emotional and moral development of children importantly includes a stage of taking increasing responsibility for all aspects of their own behaviour, and of becoming aware of the impact of their behaviour on others. "Individual development involves the capacity to integrate conflicts, to perceive people as whole persons and feel concern for them" (Trowell & Bower, 1995, p. 10). Children reach this stage by learning and internalizing from their parents over time the rules of behaviour that are necessary for people to live satisfactorily and safely together (Fahlberg, 1994). Where this process of learning and internalizing is interrupted or has not occurred, children remain vulnerable. They continue to be dependent on the increasingly unsuccessful attempts of parents to impose limits on uncontained, unacceptable behaviour, which can be aggressive and violent.

The reasons may be complicated for a parent being unable to maintain consistent control of a child's behaviour, control that the child then gradually internalizes. The reasons for this difficulty can often be traced to the parent's own ineffective or abusive experiences in childhood, possibly in this same area of development. "Every time I say 'no' to him, I sound just like my old man, which is terrifying and so I just give in and let him do what he likes."

Alternatively, the difficulty may seem to originate in a more recent and difficult adult relationship, which leaves the parent feeling vulnerable and deskilled even in relation to their own child. "He's such a control freak that he yells at me every time I raise my voice to the children and so I've given up and they just run rings round us both."

Appropriate and timely child and family mental health intervention may help prevent escalation by supporting the parents towards a different understanding of their difficulties.

As with other child mental health presentations, when a parent is struggling to manage a child's behaviour, a psychoanalytically orientated therapy approach would prioritize the formation of a therapeutic relationship between therapist and family. Through this relationship, as illustrated in the family examples below, the nature and origins of the difficulty can be explored both with parent(s) alone and also in a family context, in order to develop a new understanding that can help move towards change. Importantly, a new definition of the difficulty is sought early in the therapy, away from the problem being the child's behaviour and towards the solution being in the parent's ability to manage differently.

Family one

Greg, a three-year-old who has violent tantrums

Greg lives with his mother, twenty-three, father, twenty-two, and sister Amy, four months.

Greg is reported to have violent tantrums that are beyond his parents' control. His mother has described challenging and "defiant" behaviour and tantrums during which she gets hit and kicked, and she fears for the safety of her baby daughter. Mother reports that Greg has been like this "since day one", and says that his father also has absolutely no effect on Greg's behaviour. He listens to neither of them, though is more responsive away from home at playgroup or with other family members. "I shouldn't bother seeing him, he won't come," she added of her partner when describing her problems to her health visitor.

So at just three years old, Greg is referred to his child and family consultation service as being "beyond parental control".

Greg's mother has read about attention deficit hyperactivity disorder (ADHD), conduct disorder (CO), and oppositional defiant disorder (ODD). She is convinced that her son has at least one of these diagnoses and maybe all three: "It's just the way he is." She is frustrated and angry with doctors that Greg has not been diagnosed and given medication to calm him down and make him listen to her.

She thinks that the professionals who have seen Greg agree with her that there is something wrong with his behaviour. She feels that they have been critical and blaming of her without telling her what to do. In her opinion, they have all just been reluctant to give medication to such a young child.

Clinical intervention

Meeting one: offered to family and attended by Greg, his mother, and Amy

> Mother attended the initial assessment appointment with Greg and Amy, who was held by her mother throughout the meeting.
>
> Mother was asked what she hoped for from the meeting. Greg played and drew fairly quietly while his mother related numerous examples of his violent and impossible behaviour. She explained his settled behaviour in the meeting as his deliberate intention to "show me up" and "prove me a liar". When asked for any positive characteristics of her son, the mother simply looked up at the ceiling with the invitation "see if you can find some, that's why I'm here, isn't it?" She expressed her fear that Greg was "turning into" her own father, who had been

frightening and violent throughout her childhood. "He's even got my dad's hair." She said that, similarly, she knew of no good points at all about her father, adding only, "Well, perhaps the fact that he finally died." She explained that this had happened just before she became unexpectedly pregnant with Greg.

On the other hand, she described Amy as "a perfect baby, no trouble from her since the day she was born".

The mother agreed to request that her partner come to the next appointment, since he had not been seen by any professionals. The mother had repeatedly explained that "He's always working, that's his excuse," and anyway, "He's a total waste of space." The therapist said that she would write to him emphasizing the importance of his attendance with his family.

Meeting two: Greg, his parents, and Amy

On arrival, the father looked awkward and followed a little distance behind the others as the family walked to the meeting room. In the meeting he remained mainly silent, playing with Lego with Greg and attending to the baby when she needed her nappy changed.

The therapist asked each parent to give their view of what would help in their current difficulties. Father started to say that Greg had been very unsettled by Amy's arrival and just needed more attention and a little firmness. The mother waved a dismissing hand in his direction and silenced him with "What do you know, you're never there and now you're getting at me too?" Then she leaned over and clamped her hand firmly over father's mouth. She emphasized to him that he knew nothing and was useless even when he was there, as Greg never listened to him either. Father quietly protested that this was not quite so, that Greg enjoyed times playing in the garden and watching cartoons together. Mother quickly interrupted him with a further dismissive "Oh, yes, you're great at watching TV, but what about disciplining him, you leave all that up to me." The father sighed and lapsed into silence, continuing to play with Greg.

The referral had reported mother's experience of serious violence during childhood from her father, and also from a boyfriend when she was a teenager. There were no reports or indications of any violence in the present relationship.

The parents were offered the next two meetings alone, to which they agreed.

Meeting three: parents alone

The parents were invited by the therapist to describe what they would like for their children to be different from their own experiences in childhood.

Mother began by relating in some detail the horrors of violence from a brutal and drunken father, of which her partner already knew. She recalled with distress her own mother's attempts to protect her and her little sister from their dad, at times taking blows while the girls ran away. Her brother was never beaten, but was often present and seemed complicit. "He was my father's blue-eyed boy," she explained, "lot of good it did him, he's inside now for GBH, kept beating up his girl-friend." Of her current relationship, she said "Phil's not like that, he's a good guy but never there, and when he is, he just wants to play with Greg, never disciplines him. But he's not like my dad, don't want that for my kids, but he seems kind of weak, if you know what I mean?"

Father said that he had had good parents, but that their bickering got on his nerves. "They were never violent, not like that, barely shouted, but niggled each other all the time. I don't want that, I back off, I just want a quiet life."

Asked about any aspects of her childhood that she would like for her children, the mother replied quickly that she would like to be a good mum like her mum was. "Mum always said I was a perfect child, gave her no trouble, was a big help to her in it all, or so she said. I was OK until all these problems with Greg, didn't produce the perfect child there, did I? This is so hard to cope with now." Eventually, her mother had left home with her and her sister, leaving their father and brother behind. They moved around and did not settle down until Greg's mother was seventeen and had already left to live with her first, violent partner, Freddie.

"My mum and sister are still living in a lovely flat they got just after I left home," she said. "I don't see them any more. Mum stopped speaking to me when I took up with Freddie, she knew he was bad but I didn't listen. Then I was with Phil and had the kids. My sister's at college now doing well, I heard."

The mother stopped, looking sad and wistful, both, it seemed, from recounting some harrowing details of her early years and from a sense of loss and regret when thinking of the better lives of her mother and sister now.

Father looked towards her and looked sad, too. "And don't you look all pathetic like that," she snapped. He sighed and turned away before saying that he would like for his children that they were kind, caring parents, like his were for him. "But without the bickering, just a quiet life. I thought that's what she [indicating mother] wanted too when she left Freddie and came with me, I thought she'd had enough of fighting and would want a quiet life with me and the kids." He looked annoyed, sighed, and said nothing.

They were invited to return to tell more of their story and they both readily agreed.

Meeting four: parents alone

They were asked how they met and about their relationship over the past four years.

"Freddie was such a mistake," mother began, and spoke of his reputation as a violent and criminal young man. She had thought that she was safe with him, as no one would dare touch the girl with fighting Freddie. When asked "Safe from any man like your father?", she agreed with distress. "What I didn't see then, at seventeen, was that Freddie was just like my awful father. He knocked the stuffing out of me. I was safe from everyone else but not safe at all because I was with him."

"But you stayed with him, being beaten, for over two years?" the therapist enquired. "Yes, I had nowhere to go. I didn't see my mother and I thought I was OK with Freddie. Crazy, looking back! The beatings felt familiar, being on the alert, focusing on survival and recovery. All I knew were fear, dread, and pain."

"And the two of you met?" The couple looked at each other and smiled. "We'd known each other at school," father explained. "I always had a crush on her and wanted us to be together one day, but I didn't think she'd ever have me, I thought I wasn't her type, too quiet, too boring for her." Mother smiled again. "I knew Phil always liked me at school, he's a nice guy, maybe felt a bit sorry for me, but I thought if I'm honest that he was too good for me. I did think he was a bit quiet, he was clever, did well and had ambitions, he's got a good job now, but I get so frustrated with him, he is boring, if you see what I mean, always goes quiet when I want to talk." Father looked surprised.

"By 'boring', do you just mean that he's not violent, so no excitement? But you have been with him now for four years?" "Yes, we met in a hospital casualty, he'd been injured playing football and I was covered in bruises, he wouldn't let me go back to Freddie and we've been together since. Phil really rescued me, and I think I'm angry with him for that. It was so strange at first, quiet and peaceful with Phil, I found it boring, I missed the buzz of the fear and the fights. Then we had Greg—even as a baby he started kicking off, right from the start."

Father asked mother what she meant by wanting to talk, it seemed to him that she just wanted to yell at him and argue and that's why he went quiet. "But that makes me worse," mother replied, raising her voice. "I yell because you don't reply and you don't tell me what you think about Greg. I don't mean bickering, but I want to talk." Father looked surprised and said he had not realized, he was so afraid of arguing and had thought it would make things worse and they would get into conflict if he responded to her questions.

At the end of the meeting, the therapist offered the next meeting for the parents to practise talking and, if they wished, to think about their difficulties with Greg. They agreed to "give it a go".

Psychoanalytic thinking

After two meetings including the children, the therapist met with the parents alone to hear their stories, into which to help them place the current difficulties. First, they recounted their different experiences of family life and their respective difficulties. They recognized that remembered experiences from the past were having a negative impact on their current relationships. Despite this, they still wished to make things different for their children. This was acknowledged with the therapist.

Through the therapist's different understanding of the connections between the mother's relationships with male figures, past and present, Greg's mother comes to see that she has grown up into adult life and parenthood with an "internalized model" of violent males. First, she had a violent and frightening father, a model that she took into young adult life and replicated in her relationship with the violent Freddie. So, she had managed her fear and anxiety in relation to terrifying experiences in the past by repeating them in adult life to give an appearance of being in control of previously out of control events.

After a couple of years, apparently by chance, she moved to a new partner and, for the first time, experienced no violence, which was strange, rather empty and boring for her. She had felt rescued by Phil and resented her feeling of continuing debt to him. She picked arguments in order to be angry with him, but he backed off for his own personal reasons, which in turn provoked her considerably. She was left expressing anger for both parents, and Greg bore the brunt. Father was then able to be the calm, quiet, and reasonable one.

The couple had not been able to discuss and sort things out together because of the ill-fit of mother's inclination to angry confrontation and father's withdrawal from discussion that might lead to argument. Greg was drawn in to meet his parents' unmet needs. Mother identified violence in Greg. Father did not listen to her concerns and withdrew from possible confrontation with her and his son. The situation was clearly harmful to Greg.

The couple's relationship was also built on a rescuer–victim split. They became stuck in these roles and their relationship was paralysed. Greg's behaviour was out of their control because the parents had never managed it together. In their very different styles, neither was able effectively to set boundaries for their son.

The therapist works to reduce the splits, both between the couple and also in the strong different perceptions of the two children. When mother acknowledges her polarized feelings for the children and father recognizes his passive contribution to keeping the situation stuck, both can be supported to appreciate the real qualities and attributes in both Greg and Amy.

As well as "splitting", Greg's mother adopts the defence of "projection" to try to manage her angry, hostile feelings that could neither be owned nor expressed during her terrorized childhood and her first disastrous adult relationship. Through "projection", both parents unconsciously disown their own aggressive impulses, which feel dangerous and unmanageable. Mother does this by projecting the feelings into her son, and father is able to remain calm when his passive withdrawal repeatedly arouses an angry response in his partner.

Identification by the therapist of the parents' unconscious projections of aggressive, angry impulses is crucial in the therapy. The therapist and family can then work towards both parents being able to reclaim and express their own negative feelings, now within a safe and non-threatening environment.

By putting these feelings into words and surviving the experience, the therapist helps the parent take a step towards re-owning these feelings. If this happens then the parent's projective identification with the child can begin to change . . . from its split off form to a basis for empathy. [Bower, 1995, p. 78]

Meetings five and six: mother and father

In the course of the meetings, the couple reported that their relationship had changed significantly at Amy's birth. Mother had increasingly marginalized Phil, saying he was a useless parent, and he had marginalized himself "for a quiet life". He spent more time working, Greg showed distress, and his behaviour became worse.

The therapist worked with the parents on their being able to persevere with discussions, and even arguments, together. This took time. Father's tendency to withdraw was slowly modified as he developed trust that talking did not mean arguing, and that he could even survive some arguing. Mother was supported in regulating her emotional response so that both she and her partner could stay with and build on the discussions. The parents were clearly aided by their obvious continuing affection and commitment to each other and their family.

Continuing meetings: Greg, his parents, and Amy

As the parents were increasingly able to commit to difficult discussions, they began to think with the therapist about specific behavioural strategies for managing together their children's behaviour. They implemented the strategies with fluctuating success, and the therapy meetings continued in order to build on their successes and reflect on the difficulties, particularly of managing Greg's behaviour. Greg's behaviour noticeably improved and he seemed happier. There were no further concerns about him. Amy appeared to be thriving.

The couple continued to work together with the therapist on continuing to develop changing and rounded pictures of both children. Importantly, in adults-only time, the therapy also focused on moving the couple's view of each other from the previous polarized stereotypes. The work referred often to the past in its focus on the present.

Family two

Billy, a six-year-old whose parents drink too much

Billy lives with his mother, thirty-five. Billy's parents are separated, though his father, thirty-three, lives intermittently in the family home, where he spends significant amounts of time. Billy is his parents' only child.

Billy is referred by his social worker to child and family mental health services for assessment of risk and emotional harm. There are concerns about the effect on Billy of his parents' alcohol abuse and his father's uncontrolled aggression and violence when drunk. Billy's behaviour has become oppositional and difficult to manage. Both parents want Billy to remain in their care.

Billy's mother is receiving alcohol counselling, which, reportedly, she uses well. While her drinking can be under control, she also sometimes drinks to excess, especially when stressed.

Billy's father is described as a long-term alcoholic who, despite best intentions, continues regularly to get extremely drunk, when he can be aggressive, usually outside the home. He has on occasion hit Billy, who is frightened of his father, whom he has often seen drunk and out of control. Father has been offered help, but his attendance at the alcohol programme is irregular.

Both parents are talented musicians who used to be successful performers. They met during their musical careers when they began heavy drinking. Billy already shows musical talent, which his parents want to nurture themselves.

Billy has been in trouble at school, where he is receiving extra help with his behaviour and learning, though he is academically able. Musically, he is a bit of a star and has sung at school events. However, he has been getting into fights and has been suspended from school twice already. He can be rude and aggressive to teachers. He has difficulty concentrating on his work and is falling behind. He has lost interest in music and no longer practises.

Because of the concerns of school staff and the alcohol services' knowledge of Billy's parents, a referral has been made to social services. Billy is subject to a protection plan because of physical and emotional abuse. Social services have required Billy's mother to cease contact with father if there is any threat to Billy's physical or emotional well-being. Mother has been told she must control her drinking if Billy is to remain in her care. Legal action to remove Billy is a possibility.

Clinical intervention

The referral to child and family mental health services requests an opinion on whether Billy can safely remain in the care of his parents. Under social services protection plan, the family is required to attend the assessment.

Meeting one: Billy and his parents

> In the initial meeting with Billy and both parents at an early morning appointment, it was noted that Billy's father smelled strongly of alcohol, though did not present any obviously drunk or volatile behaviour.
>
> In the meeting Billy was mainly quiet, bent over some drawing. From time to time he startled and looked a little alarmed when his father raised his voice to emphasize a point, or even when he became slightly more animated.
>
> The therapist invited the parents' understanding of the meeting and they told some of the history of their long, committed relationship since they met over fifteen years earlier, when both were still teenagers. They recounted their time as performing musicians, when a real bond had formed between them. Despite everything and a number of separations, their relationship remained strong. They felt that social services were trying to split them apart.
>
> The therapist asked about life for them at Billy's age. Father alluded to an awful childhood, and felt that his life had changed considerably for the better since meeting his wife. "Nothing's going to separate us now," he said, shaking as he looked fondly over at her. "Now we have Billy," she replied, without referring to her own experience. "Billy needs us both." Billy did not look up from the table, but jumped as his father raised his voice. "And social services people aren't going to mess up my family now."
>
> The therapist wondered how they viewed Billy's childhood compared to their own. They looked at each other and replied that they had not really thought of it like that. The therapist invited them to do so and to return the following week.

It was time to finish, and Billy tidied up hastily as his father rose from his chair.

Meeting two: Billy and his mother

Billy and his mother attended the next meeting. The therapist heard that, after the previous appointment, Billy's mother asked father to leave home because of his continuing drinking and threatening behaviour. She said she had realized that Billy was frightened of his father, just as father had been in his childhood. She indicated that she thought she would lose Billy if father remained at home.

While Billy's mother continued her account of what had been happening the previous week, Billy played noisily in the corner of the room. He had brought with him a bagful of soldiers, which he lined up and, with loud noises of guns and explosions, he acted out a ferocious attack on some small soft dolls that he had found in a toy box. "They're all dead now," he announced, looking pleased as he laid the dolls horizontal on the floor with the soldiers standing on them, still attacking. He made stabbing noises and cries of pain, with apparent satisfaction. "They're not going to hurt anyone any more," he pronounced, victorious and satisfied, as he indicated several dolls scattered around the floor.

His mother explained how worried she was about Billy's anger and aggression, which seemed worse when his father was not there. He had been suspended from school again because of fiercely attacking a boy who called him a name. "The school can only just manage him," she went on. "He'll be on report for the rest of term when he goes back next week. I don't know what to do, he's just like his dad, lovely, but so aggressive—he's only just six." She added, with a fleeting smile, "And he's coming out on top in these fights, just like his dad." Billy looked over at his mum and raised both arms in the air, flexing his biceps with a flourish and grinning broadly.

Mother still saw father regularly and was invited to attend the next two meetings with him and without Billy. She looked surprised, but agreed.

Psychoanalytic thinking

The initial clinical formulation was made that Billy had adopted the defence of "identification with the aggressor", where, in psychoanalytic language, the ego (or the developing and functioning personality) resorts to the defence of allying with the enemy, as this seems to be protective and safer. Billy has "identified with the aggressor", his father, and become like him as a defence against unbearable anxiety about a frightening, hostile world.

Billy has taken on the violent and negative attributes of his father, particularly now that his father is no longer around as much in his life. This seems safer than remaining a potential victim and recipient of another's aggression. Billy is unaware of this process, as it is unconscious. However, he may have felt intuitively that his defence has been covertly approved by his mother, who smiles while describing his violence and to whom he displays his strength in the flexed biceps. She may be relieved to see him strutting rather than fearful.

So, Billy has become like his father. At a very young age he is bullying those both smaller and bigger than himself, but this defence against his fear is dysfunctional, and Billy gets into trouble like his dad.

However, this is Billy's way of telling the world, and especially his mother, that he is not managing. His defence importantly must be respected, or he might feel threatened and frightened until he feels safely contained by a stronger parent. If, in the therapy, Billy felt his defences were being directly challenged, he could be predicted to feel exposed and in danger. Such an intervention could be counter-productive. Previous clinical work to promote mother's authority over Billy's behaviour had been ineffective over a period of time, as Billy had simply fought his mother. Parenting support would need to be developed carefully.

Therapy with the family focuses on Billy's sense of agency, though not control, and age-appropriate responsibility, though not authority, in his relationship with his mother. He will need to learn to become actively involved in managing and then containing his behaviour, and not continuing to depend on outside figures of authority, such as schoolteachers and his mother, to impose limits for him. Therapy also builds on mother's sense of herself as an effective, competent parent who provides a safe, secure environment for Billy where he is not frightened and so feels less need for aggressive behaviours and will learn effective ways of self-control. To challenge or undermine Billy's defences directly would predictably cause unbearable anxiety for him and a repeat of the earlier oppositional backlash.

Meetings three and four: parents alone

In the first meeting with the parents alone with the therapist, mother began by telling of her own uneventful and happy childhood. She said she had always felt different from her parents and siblings and, as the youngest in the family, did not follow the others to university and into the professions. She decided to drop out and pursue her love of music.

Looking over at her husband, she continued, "And then I met Billy's dad and fell for him. He was a rebel like me, we had fun on the road and the music was in demand. Then we got in with a group and started drinking and drugs and he changed, we lost our focus and neglected the music. We had been so alike, forging our different paths. I fell for his charm but . . . you simply went astray."

Many times they had separated because of his drinking. "But he would come crying, saying he couldn't live without me, and I would take him back. We had lost the music and our lives were a mess. But when we were apart I missed him terribly and would get quite depressed. Then Billy was born."

"I felt I lost you when Billy was born," father chipped in, having been silent. "You had found a new focus and I had none. I loved Billy and our family but I felt alone and in despair. The drink became my comfort and I know I went more off the rails. I was trying to draw you back, but you and Billy left me and I had only the booze. I didn't know you missed me, I thought you were glad to be away and with Billy."

Mother looked surprised and moved. She agreed that she had found a new focus and pleasure when Billy was born, and recognized that this had given her strength to move away from her husband. She had not realized the effect on him, or that he wanted life to be different for the family and to be a part of it.

"So you had Billy and you had the bottle?" the therapist asked, "and still do? Is it helpful for Billy if you continue in this way?" The parents looked at each other, shocked, and shook their heads. They said that something had to change.

The therapist had noted mother's depression when separated from her drinking partner, of which he said that he was unaware, and asked about this. Mother described a mixture of sadness and despair when she yearned for her husband, whose presence and outrageous behaviour distracted from these feelings. She thought the feelings related to her enduring sense of failure in not meeting her own family's traditional expectations and to sadness about this.

At the end of the second meeting with parents, they decided to continue to live separately for the moment. They took seriously now the professional worries about Billy. Both wanted help to manage better, and independently of the other, the troubling feelings they experienced in relation to difficult life events, past and present. Father committed himself to a programme of treatment with his alcohol service, which would include help with his low mood and his temper, which he wanted to control. Mother aimed to rely less totally on her relationship with her husband for her sense of well-being. The parents agreed Billy would see his father regularly, and father committed to being sober for these contacts. Billy and his mother would continue therapy, with father attending also sometimes for discussion on his involvement with Billy and the family.

Continuing meetings: Billy and his mother (sometimes with father also)

The therapy task in the continuing family meetings included giving the muscle-flexing Billy a clear picture of a mother who was strong and stable enough to keep him safe. This might be in the context of some controlled social drinking. An additional task was to build up reassurance for the fearful Billy that his father was becoming a less scary person.

In her determination to keep Billy in her care, his mother began to consider again some of her talents and strengths, which she had not thought about over the years. She began to take pride in these again, though she continued to believe they were not what her family wanted for her. She had previously developed her music only with Billy's dad. She had neglected it over some years because she had always felt until now that Billy's dad was the real talent and she just "tagged along". In one meeting, dad exclaimed that he had felt the opposite: "I completely lost the music too when I lost you."

Mother had recently started a music therapy course while working part-time in a day centre, and spent a couple of hours a week as a volunteer music assistant at a nearby nursery. In family meetings she talked of these new ventures that she loved and of new friends she had made. On one occasion, in the presence of his father, Billy had looked up crossly, saying that he did not like his mum going to work and college, "and my dad does not like it either, he likes you to be at home for us." Father told Billy that things were different now, that mum could work and go to college and look after Billy too. He assured Billy that mum did not need to look after him [dad] any more, as he was now looking after himself.

With Billy and his mum alone, the therapist explored some of Billy's worries and fears about his mother having some of her own life now. The therapist complimented the mother on her talents and success in finding work and a place at college. "You have a very talented mum," the therapist remarked to Billy, who beamed and seemed pleased. "And my dad's not in trouble any more, so mum does not have to be there all the time for him."

Billy started judo classes at his school, who felt he would benefit by learning controlled aggression. "I have an orange belt now," he said, proudly. He joined a local football club, where he learned rules and told his mother about yellow and red cards. She wondered if she should start a similar system at home!

Billy began to be proud of his talented mum, who he found could work and study and also be there for him. At times, things got on top of her. She strengthened contact with her own family, who agreed to provide support for Billy if his mum went through a difficult time. Billy was reassured by this, understanding that he should not feel responsible for worrying about his mum. He agreed when his mother said that, like his father now, she did not think that he was going to get into any more trouble. During the meetings, it was reported that Billy and his dad were enjoying regular contacts together. With continuing professional support, dad had been very reliable, something he had not managed in the past. Billy told his mother that he did not feel frightened of his father any more, adding "And dad's started teaching me to play the guitar." "He's a wonderful guitar player, your dad," his mother replied with a smile.

Psychoanalytic thinking

Therapy continued over two years, at first fortnightly and then less frequently. Billy generally did well at school, occasionally getting into fights but never to the point of exclusion again. His mother was busy with work and studies. She became stressed at times. She acknowledged having drinks, though never to excess, and there were no further concerns about her care of Billy. Billy continued having regular contact meetings with his dad, which both enjoyed, and Billy no longer asked if his father was going to live at home again.

The therapy concentrated throughout on supporting the strengths and well-functioning parts of Billy's mother's personality. In family meetings, Billy saw and heard evidence that his mother could provide safe, competent parenting for him, and that he no longer needed to be fearful and aggressive.

Also in the therapy meetings, the recognition of the defence of identification by the child (Billy) with the aggressor (his father) led to an acknowledgement of Billy's true frightened feelings beneath his aggressive presentation. In this way, Billy and his parents, with the therapist, were able to move to a different understanding of his behaviour and of his true fears, both past and present.

Additionally, benefit may be gained from individual therapy for a child employing this form of defence. (See also Chapter 3).

With the therapist, the parents alone had begun to think about the split of greater hopefulness (in mother) and increased despair (in father) that began at around the time of Billy's birth. Through discussion together, and also in their separate therapies, they moved towards a different understanding and a revised distribution of these emotions, with father beginning to risk becoming more hopeful and mother moving to explore the real nature of her despair.

Summary

Work with Greg's family focuses on the parents taking back and managing in themselves the parts that they have split off into the other—importantly, father being able to reown his own aggression/assertiveness from which he has backed off when he sees it in his partner, and mother being able to manage the calmer and more vulnerable part of herself, which she attacks as weakness in Phil. They also work at recognizing the different aspects of both their children and avoiding previous *splits* of "good" and "bad". The work with Billy's family also focuses on supporting the parents in reintegrating the parts of themselves that were split off into the other, especially around the time of Billy's birth. The therapy gives Billy an increasing view of his mother as a safe and competent parent, and his father as increasingly reliable and non-violent.

The two families' stories present pictures of emotional conflict leading to splits of feelings between the parents and also of the defences of "projection" and "identification with the aggressor". Additional relevant information is obtained from observation of parent–child interactions in the therapy room, as detailed in the family examples. Importantly, from the individual family stories, the therapist seeks to understand with the parents the particular meaning for them of the child's challenging behaviour.

In both of these families, parents are seen alone as a couple for some meetings in order to consider what each is holding for the other and what changes they would like in their parenting relationship now. Sometimes, individual parents can first require space alone to think and voice their personal thoughts before sharing them with their partner.

CHAPTER EIGHT

Adolescents whose bodies bear the emotional hurt

A person's emotional or psychological state may make a contribution to a number of physical illnesses and also, it seems, may affect progress in the case of some clearly physiological disorders, such as pneumonia and appendicitis (Barker, 1979).

There is also a group of disorders, known as psychosomatic or pseudosomatic or somatoform, where no organic cause can be found for some severe, physical symptoms which are not responsive to medical intervention or treatment.

Sigmund Freud, among others, studied what he called "hysterical" symptoms in his patients. He understood these to be physical symptoms that were not diagnosable and treatable following traditional medical methods and procedures (Freud & Breuer, 1895d). The term "hysterical" has come to mean something quite different, and would no longer be used in this context.

A USA child psychiatric outpatient study reported "somatic" complaints in 11% of girls and 4% of boys, with rates between 1.3 and 5% for the occurrence of somatoform disorders (Oatis, 2002).

The diagnostic criteria for somatoform disorders were written for adults, though among this broad group of disorders, and now diagnosed in young people, are chronic fatigue syndrome and pervasive refusal syndrome.

Chronic fatigue syndrome (CFS) is also known as myalgic encephalomyelitis (ME). In 2002, the CFS/ME Working Group's Report recommended that this condition is called CFS/ME.

CFS/ME is a newly recognized and diagnosed condition where there is severe physical and mental fatigue with no explanatory physiological or mental illness. For diagnosis to be made, the fatigue has resulted in significant functional impairment of more than three months' duration. Estimates indicate that between about 0.2% and 0.6% of young people are affected by CFS/ME, and between 33% and 50% of these have another diagnosable psychiatric illness, such as anxiety or depression.

It is not known what causes CFS/ME, though the condition may begin with a cold or viral illness. Symptoms reported include extreme, enduring fatigue; headache; joint pain, muscle aches; nausea; poor concentration; sleep problems; mood changes.

In the literature on adults with CFS/ME, there is some thinking that the complaint may be a variant on depression. Antidepressant medication has been tried on adult patients. However, adolescents with CFS/ME are usually treated through paediatric or adolescent medical services rather than through child and adolescent mental health. In adolescents, the main focus of treatment is on physical rehabilitation and gradual increase in physical activity, rather than on any possible psychological component to the illness. This may reflect different thinking on the nature of the disorder in young people, for whom the treatment includes physical monitoring, gradual reintegration into age-appropriate activities such as school and socialization, and intensive physiotherapy.

The symptoms of CFS/ME may sometimes be confused with those of pervasive refusal syndrome, described by Lask, Britten, Kroll, Magagna and Tranter (1991). In this account, young people were thought to have responded to unmanageable or life threatening situations, events, or trauma by withdrawing into complete refusal to engage even in life's ordinary essential maintenance and development tasks. So, they ceased walking, talking, eating, drinking, and basic self-care, and also age-appropriate socialization and education. Nunn and Thompson (1996) proposed that the trigger for pervasive refusal syndrome may include expectable life events and associated feelings. These events and feelings are experienced as unacceptable and uncontrollable and may include actual or feared loss of loved ones, separation, health concerns, change of family location, and threat to family cohesion and happiness. When difficulties arise for a young person, a key factor in their response is the capacity to regulate and manage their emotional reaction to the situation.

Psychoanalytic perspective

A psychoanalytic perspective understands psychosomatic or somatoform symptoms or pain as the body's manifestation of feelings that have not been expressed or processed, but have been repressed as a defence against something unbearable. They are also understood as non-verbal communication of distress. A variety of unmanageable and unresolved emotions or experiences may be involved as trigger in this response, for example, unresolved and buried conflicts, painful life events, and sometimes trauma.

The body then expresses through physical distress the underlying psychic pain that has been buried and for which no other form of expression has been found. A psychoanalytic view of treatment may involve working with the patient and family to find other manageable and functional routes, such as communication through talking, for the expression of the previously inexpressible.

Family one

Ann, a fourteen-year-old with chronic fatigue syndrome

Ann lives with her parents and brother Michael, aged nine years.

Following a viral illness, she had been unwell with a diagnosis of CFS/ME for over a year, had eliminated all activity, and not been to school for almost a year. A phased reintroduction back to school had just begun.

Ann was referred to child and adolescent mental health to support her recovery and her return to school. Her progress had been slow and patchy, with small steps forward often followed by relapse. Ann attended physical rehabilitation appointments at the hospital, usually with both parents, though father contributed little and seemed preoccupied by the amount of time missed from work. He expressed concern about Ann's slow recovery. Father was described as not involved with the family apart from time spent one-to-one with Michael. Mother reported that she hardly saw her husband any more, but she did not mind as he worked hard and provided well for the family, and so they were all content.

Clinical intervention

Meetings one and two: offered to family and attended by Ann and her mother

> Mother reported that father was too busy to attend on this occasion and Michael had an event at school. Ann and her mother were asked by the therapist about family life and absent family members. They were also asked to describe the effect on the family as a whole and on individual members of Ann's illness.
>
> Ann's mother described that she and Ann were very close. She said that Ann had been close to her father as a young child but felt quite abandoned by him when her younger brother was born. Father and Michael shared a passion for sports, and spent days away together at sporting events. Ann felt that she had maintained some place in her father's affections by "pandering" to him, often running errands or offering cuddles, which he had continued to enjoy. Her mother reported that shortly before the onset of Ann's illness, she had complained to her mother that her father's expectations of her were "increasingly a pain and getting on my nerves, I'm a teenager now, you know". Her mother had laughed this off and told her that she was still her father's "little girl".
>
> A feature of family life was father's absence for long days away at his business. On the other hand, mother had been at home increasingly as Ann became unwell, and now provided full-time care for her. She was fully involved in all aspects of Ann's daily needs and health/ill health. "I don't know what I'll do with myself when she has to go to school."
>
> Frequently, in family meetings, mother spoke and answered for Ann, often using "we" even when describing Ann's health and personal

experience. When the therapist observed this back to the family, Ann tried to respond shyly for herself. She did, however, turn regularly to her mother, appealing for her mother to intervene and rescue her. Mother and daughter seemed like one.

Father was always present, though absent, in the meetings. He was reported to be upset with Ann, who hardly paid him any attention any more. The therapist heard that father complained that she was always tired and often already upstairs in bed when he arrived home in the evenings. If she was still downstairs, she would quickly say that she was tired or unwell and go up to bed. When she first did this, her father went up after her, knocking on her bedroom door. Ann refused to come out.

Asked by the therapist how this had felt for her, Ann became animated and angry in the meeting, saying again that she was a teenager and her dad did not understand. She then looked embarrassed and lapsed into a long silence.

Mother laughed and tutted, explaining that father had always liked his little girl's cuddles and attention when he came home tired. They both used to enjoy this. Now father still wanted cuddles, but since Ann's illness she had often been too tired or unwell. There had been some awkward interactions with father feeling hurt when Ann walked away on his arrival home, saying that she needed to rest.

Discussion

The situation was considered and understood by the clinical team as parents not understanding and adjusting to Ann's developmental stage of adolescence. An infantile relationship with her father was neither wanted nor appropriate any more. However, this was not recognized and could not be discussed in the family. So illness protected Ann and gave a reason to withdraw from her father.

The team considered how father could have attention and comfort, without Ann being distressed or withholding through being ill. The team thought of supporting mother in talking to father about this, or else mother might be helped to behave differently. The parents would need to find a way for Ann to be downstairs among the family and well, without being expected to provide this comfort for her father.

Meeting three: Ann and her mother (again father unable to attend)

The therapist expressed concern for father, who worked so hard for the family and truly needed comfort and "spoiling" when he arrived home in the evenings. She asked Ann's mother who she thought was the right person to provide this for the man of the house. After a long pause when mother looked at Ann, Ann put her head down and said nothing.

Mother (embarrassed): "What do you think, Ann?"

Ann remains silent with her head down and both hands over her ears.

Therapist: "Does this have to be Ann, I wonder?"

Mother: "Perhaps I could do it, now Ann's growing up, do you mean?"

Mother hesitates, looking towards Ann, whose head remains down.

Therapist (to mother, without looking at Ann): "Why not you? Is there any reason in your family why that person is not you?"

The conversation continued between mother and the therapist, with Ann clearly listening through dishevelled hair over her face.

Mother: "Well, I suppose he and I had rather drifted apart, with the children growing up and him working so hard; I'm not sure that he wants me fussing after him now."

Therapist: "Could you and he talk about this and about Ann growing up?"

Mother: "Yes, we could, I think, it's not up to Ann, is it? But I worry that he just wants his work now."

Therapist: "Though you have told me that he likes a bit of pampering too. Who will provide this now?"

Mother: "Well, me, but I'm always with Ann. I enjoy being with her and she needs me."

Therapist: "So Ann has become your companion too at present—without her you'd be alone as your husband's never there? So, is Ann expected to provide for you and her father what you are not providing for each other, do you think?"

Mother: "Now you put it like that, I see what you mean. Is that what is making her ill?"

Therapist: "We do not know what is making Ann ill. But you and your husband can try giving each other what Ann has been expected to provide for you, and see what difference there is."

Mother (nodding, and Ann looks up): "Yes, we'll give it a try."

Ann: "I'll meet my friend and leave you and dad to it for once."

Mother agrees.

Therapist: "Come back and tell me next time."

They agree to do so.

Psychoanalytic thinking

Again the theory of the "Oedipal" stage may be helpful to the therapist working with Ann's family. The theory can inform the therapist of the likely heightened anxiety experienced by Ann in this special relationship with her father, which includes long-held feelings of rivalry for his attentions. In Ann's coquettish relationship with her father she has been unconsciously in competition with her mother, and, at times, Ann would have felt a triumph over her mother. Early Oedipal issues can reoccur as a young person enters adolescence and, in the context of the parents' more distant relationship, Ann's anxiety has more recently become overwhelming.

Ann had earlier found that her viral illness had put some distance between herself and her father that she had not been able to manage when she was well. It had also brought greater closeness between her and her mother. Her protracted illness continued to serve both of these purposes. Her parents had not understood or taken seriously her complaints that her father treated her still as a much younger child, and had not adapted their behaviour to support Ann's wishes.

Prior to the next meeting, the therapy team recognized that if the parents re-established their own relationship, an age appropriate mother-daughter relationship would now need to be developed. This would be quite separate from Ann's health needs in order to support her fully in recovery and progress into adolescence. So, a focus of the next meetings was the changing relationship between mother and the teenage Ann.

Meeting four: Ann and her mother

> At the start of the next meeting, Ann said that her mum and dad had been getting on well.
>
> Mother explained that a couple of days after the last family meeting, a friend came over to be with Ann and Michael and, for the first time that either parent could clearly remember, they had gone out together.
>
> She told him that they were celebrating the "adolescence" of their daughter, and discussed with him the changing needs of Ann. "She is no longer a little girl, she is becoming a young woman now." He had understood what she was telling him and recognized that he had been treating Ann as a little girl still.
>
> Asked how she had managed without her mum, Ann acknowledged that it felt strange and a bit scary but they had talked and both recognized that Ann was growing up now and things needed to change. "We're going out for lunch on Saturday and we're going to have a good gossip then."

Family two

Joe, a sixteen-year-old diagnosed with chronic fatigue syndrome

Joe lives with his mother, brother aged eleven, and sister aged seven.

Joe was referred to child and adolescent mental health services for assessment and treatment of "any psychological aspects" of his illness. He had become unwell nine months earlier and rapidly deteriorated with a CFS/ME-type illness after a bout of flu. His whole family had flu, but the others recovered fully.

Joe had quickly become largely house-bound and very dependent on his mother for most aspects of his day-to-day care. His mobility decreased steadily as he refused all activity and failed to do prescribed physiotherapy exercises.

Joe's parents had separated soon after his sister's birth. The parents described an unproblematic separation with the children not noticing any difference as father had spent regular time away with his work. When father finally did not return home, both parents maintained that this was accepted by everyone. Joe had always been a mum's boy and was reported to have "taken it all in his stride".

A few months before Joe's illness began, father told the children that he and his girlfriend were going to marry as soon as he and their mother were divorced. "There had been no reason to do it before," mother explained. Just after Joe was first unwell, his parents completed their divorce and his father remarried.

Both parents attended hospital appointments and it was difficult to know that they were no longer a couple together.

More recently, Joe's diagnosis of CFS/ME was being queried as he was showing some behaviours more like pervasive refusal syndrome.

Joe came to the first family meeting physically propped up between his parents.

Clinical intervention

Meeting: Joe, his parents, brother, and sister

In order better to understand the parents' separation, the therapist asked the family about differences since father had left home.

All, except Joe, replied cheerfully that there was not really any difference as father was always working. Joe mumbled that he thought mum had been sad after dad left and he had been worried about her. Asked if he was still worried about her, Joe did not reply. "But she's all right now, never lonely, because she's always with Joe," his little sister volunteered, to Joe's apparent discomfort.

Joe's mother explained that she had been depressed at first when her husband left but she now enjoyed organizing her own life, as her husband had been very bossy and controlling in the marriage. She had recently realized that he was like her own mother, who had issued orders and controlled her throughout her childhood. "He's really just like my mum!" Father looked surprised and a bit hurt. "But Joe's my little tyrant now," she observed with a laugh, "now he and his illness are boss."

After a few moments' silence, the therapist commented to mother, "So now you have Joe and his illness to thank for carrying on bossing you and controlling your life. It must seem very familiar to you, after your mother and then your husband, to be so completely at someone's beck and call again?"

The mother looked startled and bemused by this comparison of her relationship with Joe to those with her mother and husband. Joe looked down, frowning.

The meeting ended with the therapist inviting the current family to attend the next appointment, to which they agreed. Father told mother that he would also attend and, after a brief hesitation, she said clearly that he should not.

Psychoanalytic thinking

The therapist gathers information and identifies two clear tasks.

1. To facilitate open emotional communication between all family members on the devastating event in their family life—the parents' separation.

The separation and very recent divorce of the parents have never been openly discussed in the family. It has been assumed that Joe has "taken it all in his stride". His feelings about this event have been neither recognized nor expressed. The therapist heard that mother had been depressed after the separation and Joe was clearly protective and supportive of his mother. At times he had been so angry with his dad that he refused to see him. Father had written strong letters to mother, citing his right to contact. Joe had then complied with visiting requirements and sulkily behaved himself. Soon after this he became ill.

A knowledge and understanding of the psychoanalytic concept of "projection" is helpful in working with Joe's family. The therapist might hypothesize that mother has managed her own feelings of anger and distress at the loss of her husband by unconsciously projecting them outwards, to be experienced and taken on by her eldest son, Joe. Joe has at first attempted to cope with the projections by acting them out through anger, distress, and rejection towards his father. When this route is blocked by his father's reference to the court order, which would cause trouble for mother, Joe becomes overwhelmed. When Joe has no available outside target for the projected feelings of anger and distress, they are turned inward and, triggered by a viral illness, his health is affected.

Through initiating conversations with the family, the therapist supports individuals in owning, expressing, and helping each other with their difficult emotions, specifically in relation to the divorce and father's remarriage. As reported by Trowell and Bower (1995), referring to Cockett and Tripp's study (1994): "One interesting finding of the study was that it was the children in re-ordered families (i.e. where parents had remarried) who suffered most" (Trowell & Bower, 1995, p. 3). The therapist acknowledges the validity of each person's thoughts and feelings about these events, and recognizes that such feelings are usual and may be similar or different for each of the children. These conversations and the sharing of experience aim to bring relief.

2. To make connections between the family's current difficulties and patterns of behaviour and relationships in the past.

Joe's illness has required his mother to be close to him, and she has given up work and many aspects of her life. She has stressed that she does not mind and is happy to give Joe the best care. Both Joe and his mother have comfortably adjusted to this new inter-dependence. However, Joe has become totally dependent on his mother again at an age when he would expect to be moving towards greater autonomy and independence.

In a telephone call to the therapist between meetings, mother said that she had been shocked to realize that she could now be allowing, or even encouraging, Joe to control her, as her mother and husband had done in the past. The therapist had wondered to her why she would be surprised or shocked, as the feeling of being controlled was one that was familiar to her. In the absence of her husband through their separation, she had felt lost and depressed. The controlling demands of Joe's illness put her in a familiar, if uncomfortable, position, and so one to which she readily adapted. The therapist invited her to consider if this was what she wanted now, or not.

Following this conversation about previously invisible, unconscious patterns of behaviour and relating, these become open to discussion. The mother began to make thoughtful conscious choices about the relationships she now wanted.

Meeting: Joe, his mother, brother, and sister

In the meeting without father, the therapist invited mother to give her view of the children's reaction to her separation and divorce. Mother replied that they had never really talked about this. She reflected for a moment. She then said that she thought Joe had seemed shocked and angry at the divorce so that his father could marry someone else. He had told his mother not long before that he assumed his parents would always stay married, even if they were not together. Joe looked up, frowning, and seemed to nod. He mumbled that he thought that was what his mother wanted.

The therapist asked mother to clarify, as Joe seemed to be speaking for her. The mother replied somewhat angrily to Joe that she was tired of Joe feeling that he had to be her spokesperson and protector. "I can stand up for myself, you know," she told him. "I can speak for myself, you don't need to keep saying what you think I'm thinking, I'm OK now and I can look after myself."

Joe looked taken aback. "Say what you think," his mother continued. "Don't keep saying what you think I am thinking." Joe clenched his jaw and clicked his fingers. "Don't know," he replied, almost inaudibly. "I don't know, I'm fed up with all this, I just want you to be happy again."

In the meeting, mother told the children that she was feeling stronger now and there were going to be some changes. "It's not good for us, me running round after you," she said to Joe. "It's got to stop and you can begin to do more for yourself, to prepare for going back to school. I can't always be at your beck and call, it's not good for you or the other two." She told them that at home she was the "boss" from now on, as it should be. She knew it was not right for Joe to "run rings round me", as he had since being ill.

From now on at home, Joe would have to wait at times like the others, while she attended to his brother and sister. She had not made him wait, she said, for several months, and his brother and sister had begun to complain. She had come to realize that family life had been organized around Joe and his illness. She was going to start sharing out her time between the three children and reinforcing household rules. She said she was returning to work part-time in a few weeks.

Psychoanalytic thinking

Once Joe's mother had understood her response to Joe's illness being influenced by patterns of control in relationships in her past, she was able to consider and change her position. Projected feelings could also be reowned after a conversation had been initiated that allowed family members to express how they felt after father left home.

Additionally, helpful information in the work with Joe's family was gained from the strong varying feelings evoked in the professionals involved. The physiotherapist working individually with Joe on his rehabilitation felt angry with the parents, whose denial of the effects of their separation she thought had contributed to Joe's illness. The psychologist working with the mother felt distressed and frustrated at Joe's apparent manipulation and control of his mother through being ill. The paediatrician felt irritated with both parents, and spoke of the mother "infantilizing" her son and of father's intermittently distancing and failing to recognize his importance to Joe.

The professionals can be understood to be experiencing feelings of anger, distress, frustration, and irritation that have been projected by family members. What the professionals are feeling may give valuable information about the experience of family members.

Summary

In the situations of both Ann and Joe, the task for the therapist with the families is to track back to their origins the feelings that are overwhelming these two young people and which may have contributed to continuing ill health.

In both cases, the young people are unconsciously attempting to sort out for their parents an unresolved and neglected aspect of the parents' relationships. In each case, this is inappropriate and unmanageable for the young person. Most difficult for Ann and Joe is that their parents had not recognized that they were attempting to rescue and support what they saw to be vulnerable parents. Additionally, both young people, in different ways and for different reasons, are attempting to avoid painful issues and situations that had seemed too much to bear. Even more difficult was the fact that the situations were so complex and delicate that they could not be talked about in the families until they came to therapy.

Mental health is not the absence of psychic pain, far from it. It is the ability to encounter it, tolerate it and develop through it. The children's difficulties are not caused solely by the overload of such pain, but rather by the attempt, for whatever reason, to avoid it. [Kegerreis, 1995, p. 107]

The task of the therapist is to develop with the families a relationship within which the unspeakable can be spoken about in order that the needs and feelings of individual family members are recognized in the families as a whole.

CHAPTER NINE

Children whose parents are "at war"

I t is well documented in the literature that children are inevitably affected, albeit to differing degrees, when their parents
separate and/or divorce.

Trowell and Bower reported on a study by Cockett and Tripp
(1994):

> The researchers found that most children were desolated when
> their parents' relationship broke down—even when those relation-
> ships were riddled with conflicts. Children showed their distress in
> many different ways: lowered self-esteem, difficulties at school,
> problems making friends and health problems. (Trowell & Bower,
> 1995, p. 3]

The variables contributing to the children's reaction importantly
include the parents' capability to protect the children from involvement in the adults' difficulties and distress, and from the separation
process itself. The extent and nature of the children's suffering may
correlate with the level of expressed or experienced conflict and
acrimony between their parents during the separation and divorce
and afterwards.

The mediation, conciliation, and Cafcass services may help to support families through the separation and divorce of parents, particularly where the divorce is protracted in the legal system and where disagreements involve the children themselves. However, the adversarial nature of the UK family law system can unintentionally intensify and exacerbate the trauma and distress for children.

It is intriguing that couples who meet and fall in love, settle down together and maybe marry and have children, can, when things go wrong for them, turn so viciously against each other. The level of hurt and disappointment is overwhelming. They may fight through the Court for possessions and money, and sometimes appear to want to tear each other apart. At times, they seem to wish to split the children in two also, as neither is able to bear the possibility that one may have a little more of them than the other.

It is not surprising that it is all so very awful for the children, as they see the two people they love and depend upon the most seeming so much to hate each other.

The children are often torn apart, grieving the loss of the absent parent and experiencing painfully divided loyalties and affections. At best, they may be distressed and confused. At worst, children may resolve their unbearable conflict by ultimately joining one parent in hating and rejecting the other.

A psychoanalytic way of understanding that falling in love can so quickly and completely turn to such pain and hate requires a look at the internal models, the internal representations, of us all as we look for a mate.

Skynner and Cleese (1983) observed in a group exercise that, unerringly across a crowded room, we head for those who exude something familiar, something we know and recognize and to which we instinctively and irrationally respond. We can be predicted to be attracted to someone from a family similar to our own, or, conversely, the attraction of "opposites" is likewise determined by our family of origin affecting our choice of mate.

These internal representations are built up from very early experiences as young infants with our primary carers and remain with us as the template by which we are led and guided in adult life and on which we develop future relationships.

Why else would a woman who has known terrible violence as a child choose a violent partner, while her sensible, rational intentions are to do the opposite? Or else she does the opposite, equally in response to the internal model from which she must flee, and finds herself with a man whom she perceives as weak and ineffectual and "not a real man", and whom she comes to despise and resent.

In the example below, both parents had clearly, though unconsciously, brought to their relationship unquestioned beliefs and assumptions about parenting and families from their experiences as children in their own families. These beliefs and assumptions remained uncommunicated in their relationship. However, they led to a number of serious misunderstandings about each other, their motives and intentions, and about their capabilities as parents. The misunderstandings led to fear and disappointment, which resulted in their separation. They expressed the fear and disappointment to each other only after their separation and while in therapy because of continuing difficulties and distress for their children. Their choice of each other as partners may be understood also as each recreating and still searching for resolution of early unresolved issues.

Family

Laura, eleven years, and Martin, nine years, whose parents continue to be at war

Laura and Martin live with their mother.

Five years earlier, mother had suddenly left the father and taken the children from the family home. They had moved around before settling in their new home a year earlier. Father continued to live not far away.

The children were referred to child and adolescent mental health services for assessment of harm to them because of their separated parents' continuing acrimonious and antagonistic relationship.

The parents had not spoken to each other since mother left, except through the Court process. The children were reported to hate their father. Previous reports referred to extremely high levels of anxiety and hatred expressed and demonstrated by both children in relation to their father. These sounded disproportionate to the children's actual experience when they lived with their father. The children claimed they remembered many terrible things their father had done, though could only repeat "parrot fashion" a couple of minor examples. Mother reported that the children would run away screaming if they happened to see their father in the distance.

Mother also expressed extremely high levels of anxiety, fear, and hatred, particularly about the children's father. She described behaviour by father that she felt explained these feelings in her and the children. They all felt that father wanted to control them in a very scary way. Mother and the children were as one in their descriptions.

It was concluded that it was harmful for the children to continue being so excessively hateful and fearful of their father, who had no other reputation or characteristics of being such a man. The emotions remained disproportionate to the family's account of causative events.

Clinical intervention

Meeting: offered to family and attended by Martin and his mother

Mother and Martin arrived, both obviously in a very anxious and pent-up state.

Laura had refused to come, as she so hated and scorned her father that she saw no point in a meeting about him. Martin gave his view also that the appointment was a complete waste of time. Unlike his sister, he wanted to come to tell the therapist what he thought and to emphasize that there was no point at all in trying to make them see their father, as they would just refuse. Mother wholeheartedly shared her son's view.

The therapist asked mother specifically what she understood to be the purpose of these meetings. She thought, and looked slightly embarrassed. Hesitantly, she explained to Martin that it was not to make him and Laura see their dad, but because people could not understand why they felt such hatred for him.

"Because he's an awful monster and I hate him, that's why," Martin repeated over and over, adding, "she doesn't know him and she's not going to change my mind." He looked sideways at the therapist. His mother smiled, as though with some approval, as Martin emphasized his words. She explained that she had not influenced the children at all in their view of their dad, but she happened to agree totally with their feelings.

At the end of the meeting, an appointment was offered for mother and both children. They agreed to try to persuade Laura to come next time.

Meeting: Laura, Martin, and their mother

A week later, mother returned with both children. Martin had assured Laura that it was all right and nobody "was going to make us do anything".

Laura said, just like her brother, that the therapist was wasting their time. She hated her father because of what he had done, and she never wanted to see him. Mother showed high levels of anxiety and fear when talking about father, and the children watched their mother carefully as she visibly shook and trembled, reassuring her how much they loved her. With one voice, all expressed conviction that father could not change. The children described him as "evil".

Discussion

The therapy team agreed that little progress could be made with the children's hatred of their father while their mother was resolute in her belief that he was a bad father and an irredeemably awful and frightening man. At present, the children would not feel safe to move from a position clearly allied on their mother's side. There were concerns that the children had so totally split their loving (for mother) and hating (for father) feelings between the two parents. One meeting was offered for mother alone to try to understand her story and to offer to meet with her and father. Father had already agreed to this.

Meeting: mother alone

Mother was invited by the therapist to tell a little of her experiences of family life. She described in her childhood a very bleak and isolated time with nothing of what she would call "family life". She left home in her late teens and ceased contact with her parents and siblings. She remembered with distress a rough and brutal father who was absent and neglectful, and described a loving mother who had inexplicably seemed devoted to this cruel man.

When she met the children's father, she had been fearful and suspicious from the outset. She felt that she needed to treat him with great caution.

Asked about family life now, she replied that, in recent years, alone with the two children, they had been very isolated and constantly fearful of the outside world. The children's isolation had been a source of concern and criticism by their father, who wanted to reconnect them not only with him but also with his family.

Mother repeated over and over criticism of the father for never having been at home, not being a father to his children, and being a scary man. She said that she reminded the children constantly that their father had "never been there", though absolutely denied that she had influenced their view of him at all.

The mother cautiously agreed to two meetings with father to discuss her feelings about him and the current concerns for the children. "I suppose I have to," she repeated, emphasizing "it will do no good whatsoever."

Meetings: mother and father

The parents were asked what of their own experience in childhood they thought they had brought to the task of parenting their children.

Father described in his childhood a kind and caring, though absent, father. He saw his father only a few times a year, as his father worked away. He had good memories of a father who brought him presents and spent fun time with him when he was at home. He was genuinely bemused now by the criticism by the children's mother that he was "never there". He thought this was what fathers were supposed to do—to provide well for their family by working hard, even if this took them away from home. He could not understand her accusations of being violent and scary. In the meeting, she showed no fear of him. He could not understand why the children hated him so much, as he always cared about them and had not been the one to leave them; he had not wanted the separation.

Mother said only that she wanted to protect her children, as no one had protected her.

The therapist asked the parents what they thought they agreed on. They recognized that both had wanted and done their best for the children, and acknowledged each other's love and commitment to them. Mother struggled with this, but with difficulty was able to recall a couple of incidents of father having fun time with the children in the past. However, she repeatedly reverted to her mantra that he was never there. Father expressed his concern at the children's current isolation from all extended family, and mother agreed that she would consider some contact with a couple of paternal aunts and cousins of whom they had been fond.

In the second meeting with parents alone, the therapist asked what each thought was the effect for them now of their very different experiences of being parented in their own childhoods. They reached some acknowledgement that their attribution of erroneous meaning to the other's behaviour had led to significant misunderstandings between them. Father thought that he was doing his best as a father even if he was away, while mother berated him for being absent. Mother felt that she was protecting the children by keeping them away from family members, which father viewed as her isolating the children.

The couple agreed to a contact for the children with their father locally. Mother agreed to support the children in this as best she could.

Psychoanalytic thinking

The parents' internal representations of parents, learned in their childhoods, are clearly present in their parenting of their own children.

From their own experience, each misunderstands the other and makes assumptions about poor parenting. Mother accuses father, leaves him, and continues in her extreme negative view of him, of which the children are well aware. Father is confused by her accusations, fear, and hatred. The therapist makes possible a conversation between the parents to increase their mutual understanding of each other's experience and of their current intentions.

From a psychoanalytic point of view, the state of mind and fearfulness of the children's mother in relation to their father is understood as the result of her "transference" on to this relationship from her primary relationship with her father. Her internalized model of that early violent relationship has transferred on to her relationship with the children's father, an objectively non-violent man, of whom she was from the beginning "fearful and suspicious".

The transference transforms the present relationship (children's mother and father) into the image and likeness of earlier relationships (mother and her abusive father, father and his absent father). This process may include some distortion of perception (perceiving children's father as a violent and abusive man) and inappropriate emotion (extreme and persistent fear and anxiety by the mother which is shared by the children, who come to hate their father, with father unaware and detached from family life). Understanding and bringing into the open the parents' predetermined patterns and responses are the therapist's first steps in addressing the family's stuckness and in seeking change. With mother alone and with the couple, the therapist began the process of disentangling the effect on the present of previous internalized relationships.

The parents organized some contact for the children with their father locally. The children played and watched their father from a distance, and the parents talked together. During these initial meetings, the children did not interact closely or directly with their father, but they did experience their parents together in a different and harmonious way. Their mother was not frightened of their father. The children did not want regular contact, but they came to acknowledge feeling less fear and hatred. Further therapy meetings with mother and the children focused on the children developing a more rounded and less protective relationship with their mother, within which they could express a wider range of feelings, particularly as they approached adolescence.

CHAPTER TEN

Perspectives and practice

Regardless of personal experience of psychoanalysis or psychoanalytic psychotherapy, therapists with families may wish in their practice to draw on concepts from psychoanalytic thinking, which can add to knowledge about the deepest sources of illness in the mental lives of children and families. Importantly, psychoanalytic theory can offer therapists with families some additional understanding of difficulty in changing, either by a family as a whole or by individual members. The central place in psychoanalytic theory of the concepts of defence against anxiety and of emotional conflict can give an important insight into reluctance or slow pace of change. The importance of containment is emphasized in more recent psychoanalytic thinking.

The pace of change will vary for different families. It may sometimes take longer—not because the family is doing anything wrong or the therapist has forgotten a vital intervention, and not because the family is resistant to treatment and/or is too ill or stuck to be able to use available interventions. As psychoanalytic theory tells us, where an individual has built defences against anxiety or other unmanageable feelings, or is troubled by overwhelming conflict of emotions, it is predictable that it will take time to develop a therapeutic relationship in which the causes of anxiety, the defences against it, and unbearable conflict can be explored before it is safe to move towards change.

Family behaviour and relationships may sometimes appear to change and move on more quickly. However, until underlying worries and fears have been acknowledged and addressed, this apparently speedy progress may be short-lived. Change from within has its own chronological scale and may take time.

There may, in the past, have appeared to be assumptions about certain aspects of family life and its structure; for example, the different and distinct roles and tasks for mothers and fathers. However, since the early days of family therapy, both social norms and specific thinking about gender roles have led to significant changes in the developing theories and practice of therapy with families. Assumptions and assignment of stereotypes are now fewer, and may, indeed, be limited to one underpinning belief: that a child needs to be loved, protected, and cared for by at least one parent or carer, with adults and children having very different roles, responsibilities, and priorities in family life.

So, psychoanalytic thinking and its practice may be helpful to therapists with families as a meaningful theory of behaviour, which contributes specific psychological insight and productive self-reflection. The therapist's task includes supporting parents to refind their ability to reflect and the family to consider their difficulties together as the child is helped to move on to healthy functioning. In order to accomplish this, the therapist's role involves creating a safe, robust space within which difficult, conflictual feelings can be expressed, shared, and thought about. This developed capacity of therapist and family to feel, think, and reflect together in the room allows the establishment of a psychic structure within which feelings can be contained and hardened defences relinquished. The therapist maintains a thinking and feeling connection to the family, while also taking a meta-position from which he or she keeps a reflective presence.

Towards the end of therapy, young people often speak of some difficulty returning to previous friendships, and may report a period of relative loneliness as their peers engage in conversations and activities in which they have no interest. This can be understood as these young people having moved on differently from peers, as they have developed experience and skills in emotional communication and psychological conversations of which their friends have no knowledge. These more psychologically literate young people will, in time, either make new like-minded friends, or require more sophisticated ways of relating within former friendships.

Psychoanalytic and family work thinking share some important beliefs and principles. As with psychoanalytic practice, at the heart of therapy with families lie the principles of compassionate acceptance and bearing of feelings, while thinking with the family and all members about the difficulties, and joining them in trying to understand what has led to the problems that have interrupted developmental progress and caused ill health. The therapist relates to family members with consideration, thoughtfulness, and compassion, and without judgement or assumption, and develops with the families in the sessions the capacity better to understand and think about the troubling feelings and difficulties. Towards the end of therapy, families sometimes report that they have had some planned family meetings at home! This indicates that the capacity to think and discuss has been internalized and can now be safely replicated in a non-clinical setting.

Importantly, therapy with families is not only about what can be discussed with words, but is also about the relationship developed and the feelings touched upon through the non-verbal communication of the transference and countertransference between therapist and family members. The therapist and family members together look at relationships within the family in the room. The therapist works with what is felt, as well as what is heard and seen, in communication with the family. The family experience it if the therapist is defended against their pain, and understands and responds to their situation only in an intellectual way. On the other hand, the family also experience when the therapist is receptive and connected to their deeply felt emotions, their despairs, hopes, and joys, and is someone who cares and, with them, seeks to understand. (From personal communication with Jeanne Magagna.) "In any case, it is not the substance of a conversation but the way the heart irradiates it that infuses it with meaning" (Vickers, 2007, p. 92).

In therapy, families can have the experience that thinking and talking together about the important issues for them can be both possible and helpful. Sometimes, it is difficult and painful, and at other times it can be infused with stimulation, revelation, pleasure, and enjoyment.

REFERENCES

Asen, E., & Schmidt, U. (Eds.) (2005). Special issue—multi-family therapy in anorexia nervosa. *Journal of Family Therapy*, 27: 101–182.

Bakalar, N. (2005). Learning through affective group experience. In:
J. Magagna, N. Bakalar, H. Cooper, J. Levy, C. Norman & C. Shank
(Eds.), *Intimate Transformations: Babies With Their Families*. London:
Karnac.

Barker, P. (1979). *Basic Child Psychiatry* (3rd edn). London: Granada.

Bateson, G. (1972). *Steps to an Ecology of Mind*. Chandler.

Bentovim, A., Gorell Barnes, G., & Cooklin, A. (Eds.) (1987). *Family
Therapy: Complementary Frameworks of Theory and Practice*. London:
Academic Press.

Bion, W. (1962). *Learning from Experience*. London: Heinemann.

Bion, W. (1967). *Second Thoughts*. London: Heinemann.

Bower, M. (1995). Psychodynamic family therapy with parents and
under-5s. In: J. Trowell & M. Bower (Eds.), *The Emotional Needs of
Young Children and Their Families: Using Psychoanalytic Ideas in the
Community* (pp. 74–84). London: Routledge.

Bowlby, J. (1989). Psychoanalysis and child care. In: *The Making and
Breaking of Affectional Bonds*. London: Routledge.

Box, S., Copley, B., Magagna, J., & Moustaki Smilansky, E. (Eds.) (1994). *Crisis at Adolescence: Object Relations Therapy With the Family.* New Jersey: Aronson.

Breuer, J., & Freud, S. (1893). On the psychical mechanism of hysterical phenomena: preliminary communication. In: *Studies on Hysteria, S.E., 2.* London: Hogarth.

Briggs, S. (2000). Feeding difficulties in infancy and childhood: psychoanalytic perspectives. In: A. Southall & A. Schwartz (Eds.), *Feeding Problems in Children, a Practical Guide* (pp. 59–76). Abingdon: Radcliffe Medical Press.

Britton, R. S. (1978). The deprived child. *The Practitioner, 221:* 373–378.

Bryant-Waugh, R., & Lask, B. (1995). Eating disorders—an overview. *Journal of Family Therapy, 17:* 13–30.

Burlingham, D., & Freud, A. (1942). *Young Children in Wartime: A Year's Work in a Residential Home.* London: Allen & Unwin.

Byng-Hall, J. (1981). Family myths used as defence in conjoint family therapy. In: S. Walrond-Skinner (Ed.), *Developments in Family Therapy: Theories and Applications Since 1948* (pp. 105–120). London: Routledge.

Byng-Hall, J. (1995). *Rewriting Family Scripts: Improvisation and Systems Change.* New York: Guilford Press.

Casement, P. (1985). *On Learning From the Patient.* London: Tavistock.

Casement, P. (1990). *Further Learning From the Patient.* Hove, E. Sussex: Routledge.

CFS/ME Working Group (2002). *Report to the Chief Medical Officer of an Independent Working Group.* London: Department of Health.

Clark, A. (2004). Sal's Workshop: Alec Clark. *Context, 76:* 43.

Cockett, M., & Tripp, J. (1994). *The Exeter Family Study: Family Breakdown, its Impact on Children.* Exeter: Exeter University Press.

Crist, W., & Napier-Phillips, A. (2001). Mealtime behaviors of young children—a comparison of normative and clinical data. *Journal of Developmental & Behavioral Pediatrics, 22*(5): 279–286.

Daws, D. (1995). Consultation in general practice. In: J. Trowell & M. Bower (Eds.), *The Emotional Needs of Young Children and Their Families: Using Psychoanalytic Ideas in the Community* (pp. 63–73). London: Routledge.

Daws, D. (1997). The perils of intimacy, closeness and distance in feeding and weaning. *Journal of Child Psychotherapy, 23:* 179–199.

Eisler, I., Dare, C., Russell, G., Szmukler, G., Le Grange, D., & Dodge, E. (1997). Family and individual therapy in anorexia nervosa: a 5-year follow-up. *Archives of General Psychiatry, 54:* 1025–1030.

Emanuel, L. (1997). Facing the damage together: some reflections arising from the treatment in psychotherapy of a severely mentally handicapped child. *Journal of Child Psychotherapy*, 23: 279–302.

Fahlberg, V. (1994). *A Child's Journey Through Placement*. London: British Association for Adoption and Fostering.

Ferreira, A. (1963). Family myths and homeostasis. *Archives of General Psychiatry*, 9: 457–463.

Flaskas, C. (1997). Engagement and the therapeutic relationship in systemic therapy. *Journal of Family Therapy*, 19: 263–282.

Fonagy, P. (2004). *Affect Regulation, Mentalization, and the Development of the Self*. London: Karnac.

Fonagy, P. (2005). The 7th London International Eating Disorders Conference Programme.

Fox, C., & Joughin, C. (2002). *Childhood-Onset Eating Problems: Findings From Research*. London: Gaskell (The Royal College of Psychiatrists).

Fraiberg, S. (1978). Psychoanalysis and social work: a re-examination of the issues. *Smith College Studies in Social Work*, 48: 87–106.

Fraiberg, S., Adelson, E., & Shapiro, V. (1975). Ghosts in the nursery: a psychoanalytic approach to the problem of impaired infant–mother relationships. *Journal of the American Academy of Child Psychiatry*, 14: 387–421.

Freeman, H. (2000). Thin end of the wedge. The *Guardian*, 21 June, G2: 1–3.

Freud, A. (1927). Introduction to the technique of child analysis. In: *The Writings of Anna Freud*. New York: International Universities Press, 1971.

Freud, A. (1936). *The Ego and the Mechanisms of Defence*. London: Hogarth Press and the Institute of Psychoanalysis.

Freud, A. (1965). *Normality and Pathology in Childhood*. New York: International Universities Press.

Freud, A., & Burlingham, D. (1944). *Infants Without Families*. New York: International Universities Press.

Freud, S. (1900a). *The Interpretation of Dreams*. S.E., 4–5. London: Hogarth.

Freud, S. (1905e). *Fragment of an Analysis of a Case of Hysteria*. S.E., 7. London: Hogarth.

Freud, S. (1909b). *Analysis of a Phobia in a Five-Year-Old Boy*. S.E., 10. London: Hogarth.

Freud, S. (1920g). *Beyond the Pleasure Principle*. S.E., 18. London: Hogarth.

Freud, S. (1923b). *The Ego and the Id*. S.E., 19. London: Hogarth.

Freud, S., & Breuer, J. (1895d). *Studies on Hysteria. S.E.*, 2. London: Hogarth.

Glaser, D. (2002). Emotional abuse and neglect (psychological maltreatment): a conceptual framework. *Child Abuse and Neglect, 26*: 697–714.

Hargreaves, D., & Tiggemann, M. (2002). The effect of television commercials on mood and body dissatisfaction: the role of appearance-schema activation. *Journal of Social & Clinical Psychology, 21*: 287–308.

Iwaniec, D. (1995). *The Emotionally Abused and Neglected Child.* Chichester: Wiley.

Jaques, E. (1968). Guilt, conscience and social behaviour. In: J. D. Sutherland (Ed.), *The Psychoanalytic Approach.* London: Institute of Psychoanalysis.

Kegerreis, S. (1995). Getting better makes it worse: obstacles to improvement in children with emotional and behavioural difficulties. In: J. Trowell & M. Bower (Eds.), *The Emotional Needs of Young Children and Their Families: Using Psychoanalytic Ideas in the Community* (pp. 101–108). London: Routledge.

Kempe, R. S., & Kempe, C. H. (1978). *Child Abuse.* London: Fontana/Open Books.

Kerbekian, R. (1995). Consulting to premature baby units. In: J. Trowell & M. Bower (Eds.), *The Emotional Needs of Young Children and Their Families: Using Psychoanalytic Ideas in the Community* (pp. 54–62). London: Routledge.

Klein, M. (1937). Love, guilt and reparation. In: M. Klein & J. Riviere (1967) *Love, Hate and Reparation.* London: Hogarth Press and the Institute of Psychoanalysis.

Klein, M. (1955). The psychoanalytic play technique: its history and significance. In: M. Klein, P. Heimann & R. E. Money-Kyrle (Eds.), *New Directions in Psychoanalysis* (pp. 3–22). London: Tavistock.

Klein, M. (1959). Our adult world and its roots in infancy. *Human Relations, 12*: 291–303.

Klein, M. (1975). *Love, Guilt and Reparation and Other Works 1921–1945.* London: Hogarth Press and the Institute of Psychoanalysis.

Kraemer, S. (1997). What narrative? In: R. Papadopoulos & J. Byng-Hall (Eds.), *Multiple Voices: Narrative in Systemic Family Psychotherapy* (pp. 41–63). London: Karnac.

Laing, R. D. (1971). *The Politics of the Family.* London: Tavistock.

Laing, R. D., & Esterson, A. (1964). *Sanity, Madness and the Family.* London: Tavistock.

Lanyado, M., & Edwards, J. (1997). Editorial. *Journal of Child Psychotherapy, 23*: 177–178.

Larner, G. (2000). Towards a common ground in psychoanalysis and family therapy: on knowing not to know. *Journal of Family Therapy,* 22: 61–82.

Lask, B., Britten, C., Kroll, L., Magagna, J., & Tranter, M. (1991). Children with pervasive refusal. *Archives of Disease in Childhood, 66:* 866–869.

Lock, J., Le Grange, D., Agras, W. S., & Dare, C. (2001). *Treatment Manual for Anorexia Nervosa: a Family-Based Approach.* New York: Guilford Press.

Magagna, J. (2005). Teaching infant observation: developing a language of understanding. In: J. Magagna, N. Bakalar, H. Cooper, J. Levy, C. Norman, & C. Shank (Eds.), *Intimate Transformations: Babies with their Families* (pp. 177–188). London: Karnac.

Millar, S. (1972). *The Psychology of Play.* Harmondsworth: Penguin.

Minuchin, S. (1974). *Families and Family Therapy.* London: Tavistock.

Nichols, M. (1987). *The Self in the System: Expanding the Limits of Family Therapy.* New York: Brunner/Mazel.

Nunn, K. P., & Thompson, S. L. (1996). The pervasive refusal syndrome: learned helplessness and hopelessness. *Clinical Child Psychology and Psychiatry, 1:* 121–132.

Oatis, M. D. (2002). *Psychosomatic Illness in Children and Adolescents (Somatoform Disorders).* New York: The NYU Child Study Center, Letter 6.

Palazolli, M. S., Boscolo, L., Cecchin, G., & Prata, G. (1978). *Paradox and Counterparadox.* Northvale, NJ: Aronson.

Palazolli, M. S., Boscolo, L., Cecchin, G., & Prata, G. (1980). Hypothesizing–circularity–neutrality: three guidelines for the conductor of the session. *Family Process, 19:* 3–12.

Pocock, D. (1995). Postmodern chic: postmodern critique. *Context, 24:* 46–48.

Pocock, D. (1997). Feeling understood in family therapy. *Journal of Family Therapy, 19:* 283–302.

Renton, G. (1978). The East London child guidance clinic. *Journal of Child Psychology and Psychiatry, 19:* 309–312.

Robertson, J. (1952). *A Two-Year-Old Goes to Hospital* [Film]. New York Film Library.

Russell, G., Szmukler, G., Dare, C., & Eisler, I. (1987). An evaluation of family therapy in anorexia and bulimia nervosa. *Archives of General Psychiatry, 44:* 1047–1056.

Sayers, J. (1986). *Sexual Contradictions: Psychology, Psychoanalysis, and Feminism.* London: Tavistock.

Sayers, J. (1991). *Mothering Psychoanalysis*. London: Hamish Hamilton.

Scharff, D., & Scharff, J. (1987). *Object Relations Family Therapy*. Northvale, NJ: Aronson.

Schore, A. (1994). *Affect Regulation and the Origin of the Self*. Hillsdale, NJ: Lawrence Erlbaum.

Segal, H. (1957). Notes on symbol-formation. *International Journal of Psychoanalysis, 38*: 391–397.

Skynner, R., & Cleese, J. (1983). *Families and How to Survive Them*. London: Methuen.

Stein, A., Stein, J., Walters, E., & Fairburn, C. (1995). Eating habits and attitudes among mothers of children with feeding disturbances. *British Medical Journal, 310*: 228–230.

Stierlin, H. (1977). *Psychoanalysis and Family Therapy*. New York: Jason Aronson.

Temperley, J. (1979). *The Implications for Social Work Practice of Recent Psychoanalytical Developments*. Group for the Advancement of Psychodynamics and Psychotherapy in Social Work.

Tiggemann, M. (2005). Television and adolescent body image: the role of program content and viewing motivation. *Journal of Social and Clinical Psychology, 24*: 193–213.

Timms, N. (1964). *Social Casework, Principles and Practice*. London: Routledge.

Trowell, J., & Bower, M. (Eds.) (1995). *The Emotional Needs of Young Children and Their Families: Using Psychoanalytic Ideas in the Community*. London: Routledge.

Vickers, S. (2007). *The Other Side of You*. London: Harper Perennial.

Walrond-Skinner, S. (1979). *Family and Marital Psychotherapy: A Critical Approach*. London: Routledge.

Watzlawick, P., Bavelas, J., & Jackson, D. (1967). *Pragmatics of Human Communication*. New York: W. W. Norton.

Williams, G. (1997). Reflections on some dynamics of eating disorders: "no entry" defences and foreign bodies. *International Journal of Psychoanalysis, 78*: 927–941.

Winnicott, C. (1970). *Child Care and Social Work*. Bookstall Services.

Winnicott, D. W. (1974). *Playing and Reality*. Harmondsworth: Penguin.

Yelloly, M. A. (1980). *Social Work Theory and Psychoanalysis*. Wokingham: Van Nostrand Reinhold.

Younghusband, E. (1981). *The Newest Profession: A Short History of Social Work*. London: IPC Business Press.